How to make

Cider, Mead, Perry and Fruit Wines

How to make

Cider, Mead, Perry and Fruit Wines

CRAIG HUGHES

A How To Book

ROBINSON

First published in Great Britain in 2012 by Spring Hill, an imprint of How To Books Ltd

This edition published in 2015 by Robinson

5 7 9 10 8 6 4

A CIP catalogue record for this book
is available from the British Library.

ISBN: 978-1-90586-282-5 (paperback)

Text illustrations by Firecatcher Creative
Produced for How To Books by Deer Park Productions, Tavistock
Designed by TW Typesetting, Plymouth, Devon
Printed and bound in Great Britain by Bell & Bain Ltd, Glasgow

Robinson
An imprint of
Little, Brown Book Group
Carmelite House,
50 Victoria Embankment
London EC4Y 0DZ

An Hachette UK Company
www.hachette.co.uk

www.littlebrown.co.uk

NOTE: The material contained in this book is set out in good faith for general guidance and no liability can be accepted for loss or expense incurred as a result of relying in particular circumstances on statements made in the book. Laws and regulations are complex and liable to change, and readers should check the current position with relevant authorities before making personal arrangements.

How To Books are published by Robinson, an imprint of Little, Brown Book Group. We welcome proposals from authors who have first-hand experience of their subjects. Please set out the aims of your book, its target market and its suggested contents in an email to Nikki.Read@howtobooks.co.uk

CONTENTS

ABOUT THE AUTHOR

Craig Hughes lives in his beloved Lancashire and over successive years of wet, damp and rain has developed webbed feet and gills. An ex-lawyer, he was always tired of those that had given up the 9–5 for the better life, until illness forced him to reassess his life or possible death. Since then he has continued with his country ways, living off the land and continually annoying his friends with tales of free food, good home made wine and an early to bed early to rise diet.

He is an NFU Ambassador and promotes the benefits of embracing the countryside, its ways and its practices. He still annoys his wife with muddy wellies, muddy dogs and a permanently proffered empty mug awaiting to be filled with tea.

Acknowledgements

Thanks to the How to . . . team for all their hard work, patience and understanding, especially of a dyslexic. To Nikki and Giles for their friendship and support. Grateful thanks to Conor Daunt in Preston and all those at Crossmoor Honey Farm in Lancashire.

Special thanks to:

Kate Callaghan for introducing me to Cornish pasties and who made rather inferior tea.

John Secarda whose seamless lyrics never fail to draw me to the water's edge; when a thousand years need to be crossed in a heart beat, your words are there. Maybe a song about tea would help, John?

Tasty Eric whose jokes never fail to make me smile, no matter how bad they are, and whose tea I would rather forget. Too milky, too sweet and could pass for chicken soup. What are those green bits, Tasty?

Joni Mitchell, as I listen to Mingus all over again and wonder, when will you make me a cup of tea?

INTRODUCTION

MEAD, CIDER, PERRY, BEER AND COUNTRY WINE

As a beekeeper and with my hand to gallons and gallons of honey, I am often asked about making mead. Many people like keeping bees and are also very interested in making mead and other alcoholic drinks.

It has always been of interest to me to make my own potions and to know what goes into them. Often in the past it was the case that breweries were local and used local materials, such as local water from the fells tainted brown with moorland peat, honey from the local bees, yeast from the village baker and earthenware pots from the local potter. Just to give you one example, in Blackburn in Lancashire at the turn of the last century there were 42 independent breweries.

Today there is only one: the Thwaites Brewery. Blackburn was ideally placed as it was able to draw off the sweet and clear peat land water and use the myriad of local products to develop a number of ales. These days, as we move to a greater level of consumerism and capitalism, we often find ourselves wanting to know more about our food and drink. What is its provenance? Where did it come from? Often we never know, or even worse we have fond notions of something being produced round the corner in a rose-covered cottage or in a converted barn in somewhere like the Lake District. But so often our food and drink are produced in a massive factory, all stainless steel and sanitised, on an industrial estate in the Midlands just off the M something or other. Sorry to kill off your ideal . . . Things do seem to be changing, though – a reversal of fortune even. Many of us are questioning the true provenance of our food and drink. Many of us are starting to delve into the delights and often mysteries of making our own food from scratch, including our own drinks, teas, beverages and wines.

I'm quite proud to say I'm one of those people who questions what I eat, drink and sometimes even what I wear. I do this not because I'm a vegetarian, eco-warrior, or environmental terrorist but because I am just concerned about what I eat and drink. If I can produce something that I enjoy, costs little, and uses up things that others would throw away then I'm a happy bunny. A lot of this depends on the balance of life. I like nothing more than a nice pork chop, marinated in my own cider and glazed with my own honey, served with my own spuds and carrots: perfect! And yes, I'll serve that with a glass of my own wine, and later have a mug of my own tea. Sounds idyllic, doesn't it? But actually you do have to remember that although it's a lot of hard work, there's nothing better than shaking the soil off your carrots, watching the rain run off your beans and peas and tasting the natural, sweet and delicious flavours pouring out.

HOW TO USE THIS BOOK

In this book I want to introduce you to some of the delights of making your own drinks – alcoholic or non-alcoholic, made from your own fruit or vegetables or brewed using a shop-bought kit, whichever takes your fancy. I'll talk you through some of the recipes I've used over the years and show you how to get the best from your ingredients. We'll look at the basic recipes, but also how to adapt and develop them according to the ingredients that you happen to have available. For example, there are many different types of mead, and all with the same magic ingredient: honey. We'll have a look at types of honey in Chapter 3, and work through the mead recipes in more detail in Chapter 9, but basically by using a different honey with a different process/product the tastes and variations of the drink can be endless. I will talk about fruit wines too a little later on in the book and you will no doubt start to think about what will happen if you experiment with this, that and the other. You will have all these natural ingredients with differing flavours and your imagination will go bonkers. No doubt you will be buying this book in the spring when it comes out. If you are buying this book in another country, like America, Canada or Australia, then you will have to bear in mind the seasonal changes and the types of fruits, vegetables and nuts that will be available to you. I would like to hear from any of you who have made a particularly interesting brew from a local, regional delicacy.

The first three chapters of the book will give you an overall introduction to brewing and its history, and look at some of the key ingredients: apples and honey. The rest of the book gives you the various recipes and methods. As we work through these, I'll also introduce you to some of the characters who have influenced my life – and my brewing! Let's meet some of them now.

My father

When my brother, sister and I were children we found, like many others, that we wanted to try 'drink'. Growing up with strict parents in a Catholic country it was difficult at times to get hold of any, but my parents were quite modern as well as strict and realised that the problem with binge drinking arose when youngsters were kept away from it. A bit like the French, who introduce their children to a red wine when they are infants, watered down of course, we gained an appreciation of drink and alcohol through being allowed a weak mead or cider. Quite often my father would make some braggot and allow it to ferment over a couple of weeks. Then on a Sunday after church and around the big kitchen table he would allow either my older brother or sister to break open a bottle and share it out for everyone. We three grew up with an appreciation of alcohol and never wandered off the path. My sister now lives in the wine-growing region of the Mosel in the Saarland and has a damn good cellar. (Sadly, my cellar only has in it a bag of old cement powder that's gone off and a mattress that smells of wee.)

My father was always one for something for free. He wasn't a miser, he just preferred something for nothing. He loved to barter. Often he would come home with a sack of Brazil nuts or a dozen cauliflowers after doing a job for someone. So when it came to home-brew he was a wizard – not because he spent a lot on equipment or kits; he didn't, he just used what was available to him. At varying times of the year, as the seasons changed he would change what he made. Among the finest meads he ever made were a blackcurrant and a blackberry (actually two separate meads, not a blackcurrant/blackberry mix). We'll look at some of his wonderful mead recipes in Chapter 9.

Hawky

When I first met Hawky (a keen fan of the band Hawkwind), I was reminded of my own youth and hippyish phase – he's a distinctive man, with long grey hair, diagonal glasses perched on the end of his nose, and a smell of patchouli oil, motorbikes and leather about him. Hawky is a lovely, kind, caring man with a real enthusiasm for his craft. He owns the Dragon's Breath Brewery, and I'm delighted to be able to supply him with honey for his brews. He's also a druid, and a formidable pagan. You'll find out more about his methods of brewing in Chapter 4.

Hélène and Franck Terminière

Now I'm quite the Francophile, loving many of the things *la belle* France offers. I am to be found, with a glass of the local vino in hand, ham and cheese demi keeping me company, a sleeping dog at my feet and my bright yellow Renault 4 gently rusting. I paint a romantic picture but life is very much like this. On a recent visit to the Dordogne, the beekeeper's wife and I pitched up at a gîte, unpacked her dreadful car and set about pretending to be French for a month. Once we visited a farmer's market in the beautiful market town of Brontôme. Pale blue painted shutters, squawking chickens, a variety of smells and the bustle of a country market all served for it to be a good day out. Halfway up a hill I spotted a lady selling miel (honey) so off I popped to try and talk to her in my very basic French. She smiled and nodded as I made exaggerated hand signs and complemented this with lots of deep intakes of breath and 'ooh la las'. At this point she said to me in clear English, 'Do you know Wolverhampton? I was an au pair there.' This came as a great surprise to me because I never thought anyone in Wolverhampton would want an au pair. This young woman was a younger version of me, but a different gender, a lot slimmer and spoke better English than I did. But I saw in her the same enthusiasm and desire to know about the countryside that I have. When I explained that I was a commercial beekeeper she almost hugged me to death. She had started out two years earlier as a beekeeper and felt like she was working alone and was worried whether she was doing it right. She invited us to her house for dinner and to meet her husband and to talk of bees. When we arrived we found a simple, pleasant French farmhouse in a neat tiny village. Hélène and Franck Terminière are a lovely couple setting off in their married lives together. Hélène asked me a thousand questions about bees, foraging, mushrooms and bread. She opened a bottle of something that she had brewed – a clear liquid made from honey and spring water, distilled over a couple of months. Sat in the shade of a lime tree, eating cheese and bread and drinking this local mead, I was at home. The month that we were to spend in France was supposed to be a time of rest and relaxation. Instead we spent hour after hour in the company of the Terminières, tasting their wines and other brews, and learning vast amounts about making these lovely drinks. I'll talk you through some of their recipes in Chapter 12.

CHAPTER 1

THE HISTORY OF BREWING

I always like to look at the history of a product. There are many reasons for this – I quite like to know where something has come from, to examine its movements, plot its path on a map, as it were. The history of brewing goes back a very long time. No one can be sure of the exact date brewing was first practised, but we do have an idea of its first location/s.

CIDER

We know that apples were referred to several thousand years ago as being grown on the banks of the river Euphrates in what is now Baghdad. The trees were not grown in a scattered mismatch approach, rather they were laid out in irrigation ditches and in the symmetry of a well-placed orchard. We also know that apples were grown in the Caucasus and in and around Turkmenistan, where a wild variety still grows. This particular apple is ideal for both eating and brewing. Over the years hybridisation has occurred and as some of the non-specific types of apples died off those that were more popular, the non-sour ones, prospered.

It has been suggested that apples originally came from China. Although there is no evidence of this (even though the Chinese are great ones for keeping records), it would make sense that apples on their way from China along the Silk Road might have got as far as Turkmenistan. It is questionable as to whether the presence of apples naturally indicates that brewing occurred; on the other hand it is certainly a possibility.

The fertile crescent of Turkey, Egypt, Palestine and the Caspian Sea has a noted amount of apples and orchards, although we have to wait until Homer's *The Odyssey*, written around 800–900 BC, for the first reference to an *orchard* to be found. I accept that this isn't necessarily a reference to the production of cider – but it would come as a huge surprise if some clever soul hadn't tried to find a way to escape from his cave-dwelling wife. (One of the easiest references to note in a garden or orchard as to whether the apples are fermenting and what effect that has on an individual is to note the actions of wasps in early autumn when fruit that has fallen has started to ferment. The wasps will gorge themselves on the fruit and steadily become drunk. Unfortunately wasps don't giggle or stagger around laughing at each other; they tend to become aggressive and sting indiscriminately.)

There are other references to the cultivation of apples, by Varro and Pliny, who both described the production and storage of apples. In the first century, Pliny travelled to England with the Roman invasion.

He noted that Kent farmers would auction their fruit whilst it was still on the trees, and this is still in practice today in some of these Kentish orchards. So it becomes difficult to identify exactly when these fruits were first used to make cider and when exactly orchards were first planted to create a surplus of apples. We certainly know that apple trees were planted and orchard development took place in Roman times in England, as it was recorded by Roman historians. Traces of apple orchards have been found in Bermondsey in Kent and as far north as the shaded valleys of Doncaster, as apples were easy to grow in many parts of the United Kingdom. Roman soldiers were given a plot of land and encouraged to farm it. Encouraging the planting of an orchard was a clever plan by those in command as, if a Roman soldier wanted to benefit from his investment, he had to wait several years for the trees to produce fruits. This was therefore a way of encouraging the soldiers to put down roots in more ways than one.

The UK has been the crossroads for many nationalities over the years, for example when the Romans left, a number of new armies and cultures came to settle here. Amongst these were the Saxons, Danes and Jutes. This appeared to lead to an abandonment of the orchards, largely because these invading forces believed that anything associated with the Romans was associated with ghosts, so they stayed clear of the roads, buildings etc. and the orchards suffered the same fate. Yet these armies were not teetotal and brought with them their own styles and brews.

As the orchards fell into abandonment the trees grew wild and hybridised. With the establishment of Christianity in England, it was the monks and their cloistered lives, walled gardens and scientific approaches that led to the development of mead and cider. From the period of the Viking invasion and conquest the monasteries and abbeys were able to develop the ideas of growing and harvesting fruits, not only for eating but also brewing. The monasteries of Ely, Canterbury and Lindisfarne were famous for their orchards and by 1275 records appeared of cider for sale to the public from the monks of Battle Abbey in Sussex.

When the Normans had come for a day out and never left, the United Kingdom not only became a divided society, but also had a new language as the official tongue and the cultural practices of the Norman French became commonplace. These included the use of apples and pears for cider making. Since then cider has been seen as primarily an English drink, although from the Belgian lowlands right the way through to the Breton coast and even up into Flanders and Southern Holland, the use of pears and apples for brewing is commonplace, and one of the leaders in apple production for cider is the Irish.

MEAD OR HONEY WINE

Now what is it about mead that leaves us with a warm feeling in our souls; a feeling of warm nights beside a roaring fire, crackling logs and a ghostly mist at the window? It's a drink for autumn evenings perhaps? Yet as a beekeeper I've been involved with mead for years and the amount of people who embrace thoughts of mellowness and golden falling leaves are many, but those who have tried it and who are keen drinkers of mead are few. And it's a shame because it is a beautiful drink that is crisp, clear and smooth. Mead is diluted honey and water, which has been fermented by yeast. As simple as that.

Mead is one of those drinks that people feel they know about but can't be sure whether they have tried it or even like it. What is clear is that mead has been around for a lot longer than cider and has crossed a number of cultures and distances on its journey. We know that mead was drunk in China around 7000 BC. The drink was popular amongst the Vedic people of India and features enormously in their religious practices. In AD 60 a recipe was written down by Columella (the most important writer on agriculture of the Roman Empire) for the production of mead. We also know that mead features in folklore and myths from the Urals to the Atlantic. It is mentioned in *Beowulf* and found in most European cultures. It was especially popular in northern Europe, where grapes were not grown. Claude Levi-Strauss noted that the invention of mead is a marker of the passage 'from nature to culture'.

Mead is one of the oldest alcoholic drinks, the recipe for which has been passed down through the generations and hardly changed over the years. Some additions have made their way into it but on the whole it's relatively untouched. What we have learnt from early societies and cultures is that people generally drank mead or braggot because they were safer, because of the fermentation process they had both been through. The fermentation process generally removed anything nasty and provided a safer alternative to drinking water, which up until the past 100 years in some parts would be contaminated with cholera or other waterborne diseases. Fermentation would remove these or at the very least, temper them.

There is a lot of folklore surrounding honey as there is with mead. As far back as the Vikings, it was believed that mead could influence the outcome of a birth. It turns out that they were right. Mead is essentially a mix of acid and sugar, and that mixture influences the pregnant mother's acidity, which in itself can influence the sex of the child. (Those clever old furry Vikings! It's no good if you're a Viking and Mrs Viking keeps having girls. You need boys for pillaging.) The making of mead has always been seen as magical. It's fairly magical now, but in the old days the turning of honey and water into an alcoholic drink was only allowed to be conducted by the pagan priests – the recipe being secret and given to them by the pagan gods.

Braggot is a drink which uses a combination of mead and grain to make a weak beer. From the fifteenth century right the way through to the eighteenth century the main body of the population couldn't afford to drink wine so they would drink braggot. As mentioned above, as the local waters were generally contaminated with a variety of waterborne diseases, braggot would in fact be the safest drink because it had been fermented. When you see a drunken group in a seventeenth century play, swilling tankards of ale around, they would actually have been drinking braggot. Ale would have been too expensive and potent to drink whilst working, mead was really for the well-off and not seen as an everyday drink, and wine was only for the wealthy few.

PERRY

Perry is a similar drink to cider but made with pears. There is a marked difference between using any old pears and perry pears. If it's quality and taste you are looking for it might be best to consider the use of perry pears, or if you are considering making a pomagne you may wish to use up what you have lying around at the end of the summer.

CHAPTER 2

APPLE VARIETIES

What you have to realise is that your cider quality depends on the type of apple you choose. It's not as easy as just grabbing any old apples. You have to carefully select the apples for your brew. I do know of people who have used a variety of windfalls, crabs and bruised eating apples. But in fact, the best cider is traditionally made with 33% each of sweet apples, bittersweet and sharp, if you are to get that traditional flavour and strength. Otherwise you will end up with essentially a sweet fruit juice that may be alcoholic – a bit like the fruit juice you buy in the supermarkets, sweet and sticky. Mind you, you might want that, but I find most people actually want something that's on a traditional format. This is where it begins to sound a bit scientific. The main characteristics of a cider apple, which contribute to the classification, are the phenolic compounds (or tannins) and the acidity. Bittersweet apples contain 0.2% of tannins and less than 0.45% acidity, which is calculated as a malic acid. On the other hand, sharp apples have less than 0.2% tannins and greater than 0.45% acidity. Sweet apples have less than 0.2% tannins and less than 0.45% acid. So it is a balancing act to get that distinctive flavour.

There are so many varieties of apples, not just in your own native country but far and wide. As the world's most popular fruit its cultivation and development into new varieties continues. Having said that, the range of apples ideal for cider making is now much more limited than ever before. Sometimes you can find a tree abandoned in a field, on a farm or at the side of the road. Planted many years ago the tree has grown wild and would benefit from being pruned and its fruit picked. These days there are around ten or so varieties of apples grown for cider making, which isn't a lot and doesn't offer the choice for the prospective cider entrepreneur.

APPLES ACCORDING TO TYPE

You will see from the following sections that there are far fewer varieties of bittersweet apples than of any other type. However, if you are making single variety apple cider, these are the apples you would use to achieve the best cider. Most modern cider makers, making cider in the traditional manner, will use one or more varieties of bittersweet apples.

Bittersweet apples

These give the traditional English cider its true range and flavour. As its name implies, the fruits are quite low in acid and rather high in tannin. Often cider makers will not look for a single apple to use in the cider making process but will look to use a combination. I have found that to get the right balance it is better to experiment. The nature of your local water – i.e. how hard or soft it is – will dictate which apple varieties are best to use. That is, unless you choose to use a still, bottled water. Over the years I have found that **Tremlett's Bitter**, **Dabinett**, **Yarlington Mill**, **Fillbarrel**, **Harry Master's Jersey**, **Knotted Kernal**, and **Kingston Black**, to name a few, work really well in cider making. Try playing around with apples and flavours and you will be surprised at the results.

Bittersharp apples

I wanted to show you the list of bittersharp apples here, but actually the range is so wide and varied that I don't think I can do it justice. Instead, here is the address for a web page on which you will find a vast list on all the apples that are classifed as bittersharp: http://homepage.ntlworld.com/scrumpy/cider/apple2.htm

Sweet apples

The list for sweet apples isn't as long as those for bittersweet or bittersharp. What I can say, though, is that although you might struggle to get even a small selection of the bittersharp apples in your local supermarket, the sweet ones are to be found there all year round and in abundance. Apples with such common names as **Gala**, **Golden Delicious**, **Braeburn** and **Fuji** can be found anywhere anytime. It is doubtful whether you would use these sweet apples in cider but you might wish to experiment with flavours and levels of acid.

CHAPTER 3

TYPES OF HONEY

As a beekeeper I've known for a long time that honey isn't just honey, it differs from plant to plant, from region to region. Honey from the Yucatan region of eastern Mexico is dark, rich and has a slightly crystalline texture and a beautifully rich floral flavour. Placing this into a mead mix might work very well – I say might, as I've never tried it before, but I would tend to think you could experiment with all sorts of varieties of honeys. I have supplied a wild flower honey for a blonde beer made by my local brewer. Many barrels and pints of sparkling yummy beer later, it was a hit. A wild flower honey will differ from region to region. Let's take a county like Lancashire; your wild flower honey will change in a variety of ways from one side of the county to the next. On the hillier side of east Lancashire your honey will have heather from the hills in the latter part of the season, and from the lower areas of the fells a rich dark almost molasses type of honey will be drawn from the broadleaf trees and the hedgerow.

And yet travelling over to the west of the county, not that far away from our original east Lancashire, we find that the flowers on the west coast are more varied and delicate: poppies, rape seed, borage, clover and beans, as well as the hedgerow and broadleaf trees. You will find that this type of honey is a clear honey and one that makes a fantastic addition to your brew. So it's not clear cut to think that using a honey in mead or beer will produce the same effect every time. I guess that's the beauty of experimenting with a variety of honeys. Sometimes you just don't know what you are going to end up with. I once tried using a fabulous honey from the Middle East and I will tell you of that later.

MANUKA

This is a well-known honey that comes from New Zealand. It is a popular honey that is high in antiseptic qualities. It's also high in cost, unfortunately. Some manuka honey is incredibly expensive and this is due to the limited availability of the plant. It is a rich deep honey that has a beautiful aroma and the flavours of caramel and toffee. It's a wonderful full-bodied honey, that is thixotropic and won't set nor run, a bit like the Australian jellybush honey from Queensland. The jellybush produces a honey similar to manuka and similar to heather as it is from the same family of tea tree. All of them are high in antiseptic and all have a very similar taste and consistency.

MEXICAN YUCATÁN

This is a very sweet honey, deep dark and rich, and it has a high sugar content. If you leave it to cool for a while the sugar crystals become large and sharp and make eating the honey quite a challenge and painful if you get it wrong. But using this as an influential and integral part of your brewing process will enhance what you choose to produce.

CANADIAN WHITE CLOVER

This is a medium-range sugar content honey with a pure brilliant white colour. It is set and will need to be warmed gently if you wish to add it to your mix. It has a floral flavour and smell and will infuse your mead or beer with this flavour. It isn't delicate but it's not strong either; it gives a gentle infusion to what you are producing. It's not easy to obtain but is a useful addition and a good all-rounder. This is very similar to Egyptian White Nile clover honey. The Nile honey is a lot harder, or set, than the Canadian clover and this maybe because of the influence of the cotton on the banks of the Nile combined with the clover. But it is still a great addition.

DATE HONEY

Some years ago I visited Yemen. Even then it was a dangerous place, not somewhere you went for a jog after 6 p.m. let alone at midnight. I used to go for a run after midnight in the summer in New York – I would disappear for hours around Central Park and the reservoir – until I discovered that a run in Sana'a in Yemen was actually safer than running in Central Park . . .

I was in Yemen at a conference for Middle Eastern beekeepers and commercial honey producers and we were all in the capital, where the producers had their stalls brightly set out and displayed. I ventured amongst them with my smattering of Arabic and was presently surprised to meet a man who looked like Prince Naseem Hamed the boxer. We chatted in broken English and then he offered me some honeys to taste. They were all fabulous, truly. As he turned his back to deal with something, I stuck my finger in a very dark, sticky, almost molasses-like substance. It was beautiful. Dark, almost black, slow moving and sweet, with a hint of what can be best described as treacle. As he turned around he saw me and exploded; he hit the roof. He was very, very angry. I smiled and tried to figure out the problem, but it was then that he started waving an AK47 around and with a fierce look on his face started banging the table with the rifle's butt.

A friend of his came over and tried to calm the situation down. After a lengthy explanation the friend explained that the issue was that the honey that I had tried and really liked was in fact honey destined for camels, especially young camels and sickly ones. He was annoyed that I had tried all of his honeys and decided that the cheapest, most unworthy honey destined for livestock was in fact his best. Quick as a flash I told him I had a herd of camels on the beach at Blackpool and I was looking at importing honey from him for my new enterprise. This seemed to work and I took a big bottle of date honey home with me, along with his business card and the blessing of Allah. You've guessed it. I came home and made some beautiful beer and mead with only a small amount of the date honey.

TASMANIAN LEATHERWOOD

This is one of my favourites as it has a beautiful, almost caramel, cream bordering on butterscotch flavour; a set honey, creamy white with a very smooth texture. This honey will lift the flavour of your brew to give it a unique taste. It is widely available and fairly inexpensive.

AUSTRALIAN EUCALYPTUS

This is another beautiful honey from down under. But this one has that sharpness to it of the eucalyptus tree. This is sharper than the tea tree and has a more powerful kick and flavour.

Now I could go on and on about different types of honey, their benefits, varieties, flavours and price etc., but just listing honeys is not what this book is about. Just enjoy yourself experimenting with them and try to find the one that suits you in every way.

CHAPTER 4

MAKING CIDER – HAWKY'S WAY

I first met Hawky at a talk I was giving on beekeeping. Desperate to become a full-time brewer and desperate not to drink his entire brew, he was at the talk because he wanted to find a supplier of honey and, luckily for him, he met me. Hawky then took me on a journey of discovery along the lanes and byways to spot suitable ingredients for brewing, and he described to me – with great enthusiasm – his method of making cider.

COLLECTING APPLES FOR FREE

He explained that to keep his costs down he would only ever take free apples, and offered a service to his contacts and friends where he would collect the windfalls and pick from the bough. From this, he explained, apart from clearing the gardens of rotting apples he was also getting the best for his cider.

'I have a system', he explained. 'I have two wheelbarrows,' he said (such decadence, thought I). 'One wheelbarrow takes the bough apples and the other the windfalls. Apart from avoiding any cross-contamination of stock, I am able to single out the good from the bad. The windfalls all go off to my pigs. Apples and acorns; pigs love both. So for next to nothing I am able to feed and fatten my livestock, get a good taste to the pork, clear my friend's garden, get fit and get to the first stage of brewing for little or no cost. I always make sure that I give a generous amount of apples to the household as a thank you, and some cider or mead.'

AVAILABILITY OF INGREDIENTS

'It all depends on where you live and what's available,' said Hawky. 'I often have a walk around some of the country lanes. I have a look at what's in the hedgerow, often it's only old tin cans, but sometimes you find beautiful elderflower, summer and autumn fruits, hazel or filbert nuts, and often you will see some wild apples growing, not crab apples, but a mixed variety. Often you will see a house with several fruit trees, like pear, plum and apple, and I ask the owners of their intentions for the crop. More often than not than not they just let them fall. I offer my free service of collection and I'm in business; once you are in you are in forever. I've been going to one house for 20 years. We are the best of friends now.'

After he had shown me some of the different type of trees available for cropping we returned to his micro-brewery, no more than a converted garage, kitted out with hot water and wipeable floors and walls. He then took me through the process.

BREWING CIDER

'Firstly,' he said, 'you have to rub your chin, and mutter something about "I could just go and buy it from the supermarket". Then you remember just how satisfying, crisp and clear your own cider tastes. I always make sure that the fruit I use is fully ripe – you don't want any that are too heavily bruised or have any muck or rot on them; if that's the case, then they are for the pigs. Don't let anyone try to palm you off with any really old nasty fruit, because you will need to leave it to mature for at least a week to allow the natural sugars to develop. I always leave the fruit for a couple of weeks in a nice dry and cool place, like the garage, garden shed, or a barn. At one time I used to leave them in my girlfriend's living room (or, should I say, my ex-girlfriend . . .). A barn is fine, but you don't want the apples to attract a bundle of hungry mammals. Over the years I've brought home a number of chest freezers that were being thrown away. They are ideal for keeping fruit in as they let in very little air and they keep the fruit safe and secure. I also like the fact that the people who own them are usually happy to give them away as they are no longer of use to them. Bingo, everyone wins.'

FURTHER PREPARATION

'Once you have selected your apples, make sure they are washed thoroughly and that any insects are removed,' Hawky continued. 'You find often there are little grubs that live in the apple and often these are best viewed by cutting the apple in half or quarters. Don't go along with people who say "it's only protein"; it's not. It's a contaminant that can react with the fermentation process and cause a lot of sickness. Also, have a look at the top and bottom of the apple and check there aren't any slugs in there.'

'One way of removing insects easily is to give your fruit a saline bath. This is especially useful when using hedgerow fruits. All the grubs and moveable proteins will work their way to the surface, then you can just drain off and discard the liquid. Don't use too much salt though as that will affect the natural yeasts and fermentation process. You really don't want any soil on the apples, but if you follow my "two wheelbarrow system" this won't be an issue.'

CRUSHING THE FRUIT

Hawky went on to say that when it comes to crushing the fruit, he actually likes to cut each apple up into halves or quarters. This then makes it easier for him to crush the remainder. It also allows him the opportunity to extract as much juice out of the apples as possible. 'In the past,' he said, 'I've used everything and anything to mash the apples, from a rolling pin, to a piece of wood, to a metal pole. But it buggered my hands up," he said. As he makes lots of cider he has invested in a crusher, sometimes referred to as a Scratcher, which is not too expensive and does the job for you very well. The crusher is literally a hopper with acid-resistant alloy blades that always look new after a rinse. These are turned manually and the process will render your apples into a pulp referred to as a 'pomace' or 'pommy'.

PRESSING YOUR PULP

You should at this stage have a 'bulky pulp', as Hawky describes it. It will now need to go into a press. He showed me a selection of home-made presses, including his massive pumping machine . . . his pride and joy, bought for only £200 brand new. It is essentially a racking system that uses pressure to extract the juice, and can press 20 litres at a time.

CHECKING THE PH

It is important at this point to check the pH of your juice, as too high a pH will destroy the fermentation process. The range should be between 3.9 and 4.0, but don't worry as that is a huge area for movement. At this range you will find the sharpness you are looking for. You can check the pH by using a small soil-testing pH meter. If the pH is too high you can lower it by adding a quantity of precipitated chalk, and if it's too low you can add some malic acid to control it.

CHECKING THE SUGAR LEVEL

When dealing with this area you should check the specific gravity, or the SG if you like to be with it, with a hydrometer for your sugar levels. To get a really potent cider – something with a kick like a mule – you really want to be looking at 15% sugar, which equates out to a specific gravity of 1070, thus giving a total alcohol content (or ABV) of 8.5%. I am presuming it's the alcohol you are after and not just apple juice. Then, if you want something a bit more quaffable, with less of a kick to it, you will need to lower the sugar level and decrease the SG. By lowering the sugar percentage to 10% this will give you an alcohol level of 6%. But remember this is if all the sugar is fermented, and that is a key issue. You may find that the specific gravity level is less than 1040; if this is the case you will find that there may not be sufficient alcohol to protect the product during storage. If you can raise the gravity by adding sugar, say about 60g, this would raise the alcohol content of the product to around 5%.

THE FERMENTATION PROCESS

With great delight, and with the enthusiasm of a ferret in a pantry, Hawky went on to explain the fermentation process. He explained that the juice now needs to be poured into the fermenting vessel, suggesting that you should only use an unmarked vessel, and one that is of good quality as a poor scratched one would harbour material and foreign bodies likely to cause a souring of the product. I could see his eyes light up when he spoke of this part of the process. 'It's not far now,' he said. He chose to use a food grade plastic container, but he said you can use metal, plastic or wood, as long as it isn't too damaged.

At this stage he covered the container with a cloth, not too tight and not so loose that it dangles in. Fermentation can be vigorous to violent at times, so you don't want to restrict the process too much. Once it has had its say and calmed down, you should top up the vessel with either more water or juice. You will need to exclude the air at this stage by fitting an airlock to the container. You won't need to add anything at this stage, as the apple juice will turn to cider all by itself – well, the natural yeasts in the apples will turn the sugar into alcohol, to be more precise.

You can control the fermentation process by adding a Campden tablet, or to give it its scientific name, sodium metabisulphite. This will kill off any natural yeast, which may run away with the process. Nature's a strange beast. Once the Campden tablet has been added you can then kick-start the process off all over again by adding wine yeast. This might seem strange, to kill off natural yeast and then replace it with synthetic or unrelated yeast, but this is a controlled substance. You will be able to control the specific gravity and the strength of your brew, and time the process, purely by using this wine yeast.

HOW LONG TO WAIT?

Hawky then took me into an Aladdin's cave of sounds. In this darkened corner a variety of plops and gurgles could be heard as the different fermenting ciders sang out to each other. They were all kept at a steady 15°C. I asked with anticipation how long he kept them for. Each barrel had two dates on, its conception and birth date, as it was explained to me. The process itself can take anything from ten days to ten weeks. Hawky let me taste a ten-day-old brew against a ten-week-old and against a two-year-old. Like wine, they just got better with age.

THE RACKING PROCESS

Hawky stood over a particular barrel. 'This one,' he explained, 'is done'. When the cider has finished its fermentation process you must check the SG and, if it is below 1005, it's time to rack the product. You do this by siphoning the cider into a clean container and all the time making sure none of the sediment or rubbish is transferred over. Then fill your new container to the top, fit a new airlock and leave it to clear. Some ciders tend to be cloudy and full of bits. Don't be discouraged by this, as scrumpy is a fine product. Leave your brew in a cool dark area to settle further. If you find that there is a repetition of sediment, repeat the process all over again until you have a clear brew. When you have reached a stage of racking that you are happy with, you should add one Campden tablet per gallon (*for those of you who work in metric, don't, it will never catch on*). The Campden tablet will stop the cider from spoiling.

BOTTLING YOUR BOOTY

When you are happy that the product is ready (that is, it's clear, there is no sediment and it's not racing around), bottle it in whatever size of bottle you are happy with. Old plastic bottles are fine as they have a tendency to move with the contents. If you use glass bottles, you have to keep altering the caps as the fizz expands.

Sit with a damp spaniel by an open fire and drink copious amounts of home-made clear crisp cider talking rubbish with your friends until finished.

CHAPTER 5

MAKING SCRUMPY

Often people confuse cider and scrumpy, and if you are the type of person who might, then you could be in for a difficult time. Sometimes people refer to scrumpy as a traditional, or 'real' cider. It is common in the cider-making counties of the West of England and in the South and South East. Obviously these are the counties where there is a tradition of growing apples, and yet as the climate is warming up we are beginning to see an abundance of apple and pear orchards sprouting up in some of the more northern counties. The area from Devon to Herefordshire appears to include the truest of English counties for making cider. But don't be fooled that it is an English discovery. They have been making cider in Ireland for a very long time and it has also been around for centuries in Normandy and the Benelux countries. There is a strong argument that cider, or cidre, was in fact a French/Belgian creation and was brought over with William of Normandy. It doesn't matter who invented it – it's bloody good.

I read an interesting piece recently as I was unsure where the word 'Scrumpy' came from. Apparently it comes from an Anglo-Saxon word 'scrimp', meaning a withered apple, and from that we get the verb to scrump. And yet certainly in the English language 'to scrump' has come to be used in several ways. (I once heard a comedian in Liverpool say that they used to go scrumping in Liverpool but not for apples; for cars.) The verb to scrump originally meant to go collecting windfalls.

You'll find that there is a marked difference between these apple drinks. Scrumpy is fermented via nature as it is made using whole apples, rather than the juice of the apple from pulping. It contains no added sugars and has no unnatural carbonation. Hawky and I have tasted some like this that can be very strong, has a tendency to be cloudy and on occasions has bits and pieces in it. I've come across it with pips and skin and lumps in it – it was the unidentifiable lumps that concerned me. It is very different to the clear or golden fizzy sweet/dry stuff you get offered at your local watering hole.

BASIC SCRUMPY RECIPE

If you want to make your own scrumpy, here's how you do it:

Ingredients

10 litres water
30 g root ginger (bruised)
The juice of four unhappy lemons
3.6 kg apples (any sort are fine)
Cup of tea whilst working

Method

Wear only the oldest pair of faded to grey once white underpants and one slipper, the choice is yours – and nothing else. Cut all the apples up in a rough fashion but don't use any metal. You can use a ceramic blade if that helps, or break apart with your manly fingers. Place the apples with 9 litres of boiling water in a brewer's bucket. Leave for a fortnight. Occasionally crush the apples with a wooden spoon. Keep an eye out for any mould forming on top – if any appears, remove it and ditch it. Keep the same grey underwear on at all times. If your wife asks any questions tell her the voices told you to do it.

Boil some more water – about a litre – and pour a small amount over the lemon juice and bruised ginger, allowing the liquid to pass through and into the brewer's bucket. Give it a damn good stir and make sure it's all mixed up together. Pour the rest of the boiling water into the bucket and leave it alone to stand for a further fortnight. If any scum rises, skim and ditch it.

The next stage requires your drinking friend. Make sure he is wearing similar ancient underwear and the other odd slipper, on his opposite foot to yours. He can wear a knitted hat at this stage. Strain the brew and bottle in resealable bottles, put the tops on and leave for two days. After 48 hours give the bottles a half turn and that should fully close the tops. Retain the grey underwear! Around five to six weeks later, check the stoppers, re-tighten if necessary and lay the bottles down for around eight weeks. Wherever you leave them you must ensure it is cool, dry and darkish place.

You must leave the underpants on at all times. When the time has passed and your scrumpy is ready to drink you must invite your friend around again, with his slipper, hat and suitable underwear, and drink your scrumpy in a garden shed. This will convince both your wives you are bonkers and they will leave you alone. If they don't then the smell of the four-month-old undies will prevent them from gate-crashing.

TURBO OR BOOSTER CIDER

Now if you are the sort of person who can't hang around for several months wearing only some old, baggy, off-white underpants and a knitted cap, I can recommend the speedier version of scrumpy. Some people have been known to refer to it as Turbo or Booster Cider and I'm sure you can understand why it's been given this name! This type of cider is very easy to make and matures quickly – and you won't need the underpants at all. You use pure apple juice as opposed to whole apples. This really removes the messy side of things as well. So your ingredients are as follows:

Ingredients

4.5 litres apple juice, pure not concentrate
1.6 g packet of yeast
Sugar or honey to flavour, as per taste

Method

Pour three litres of apple juice into a clean demijohn but make sure that you have sterilised everything you need beforehand. Add the yeast to the demijohn and give it a good shake so that the yeast is combined thoroughly with the apple juice. Slap the airlock in and give it around 36 hours to ferment and do its business. Add the rest of the apple juice and leave it to continue to ferment. The only technical side of this is to ensure that the starting gravity remains the same for at least three days. You can check this with your hydrometer, which we spoke about earlier. If you like a cider that blows your head off, add around 80 grams of sugar and a couple of teaspoons of runny honey. This will give you a cider with an ABV of around 7–8%. Three cheers for Booster Cider.

CHAPTER 6

MAKING YOUR OWN INFUSIONS

I really wasn't going to do anything on infusions here, and yet I do think they belong within this book. I'm mad keen on foraging and making something to eat from nothing, or even better, making something to eat or drink for nowt. (To those of you who don't understand Yorkshire dialect, 'nowt' means nothing, or for free in this case.) Infusions are always super, and are especially so if you have been able to make them from something you have found. I'm not talking about a tea infusion of roadkill, but I'm talking about tea that may be infused with some nettle syrup or a vanilla pod. Initially, infusions were used for medicinal purposes and were mostly herbal in origin. You can actually use a variety of flavours to create your infusion but you shouldn't go for anything too overpowering. Sloe gin is a lovely infusion, as is blackberry vodka. On my hunts and haunts around the autumn hedgerow I often find things of interest and the sloe berry isn't that uncommon. It is the berry of the blackthorn. It's usually ready towards the beginning of September but sometimes is used as an autumn/winter indicator if it arrives in the latter part of August. Sloe gin has a beautifully rich and vibrant taste and colour, but it's best served carefully whilst avoiding wearing anything white – if you spill any it stains very badly.

VODKA INFUSIONS

Vodka is a good medium to use for your infusion, as it is usually flavourless and holds the medium well. If you look at the sheer number of vodka infusions that are available these days you will get an idea of how popular they are. I've seen everything from pomegranate to bubble gum flavoured vodka. Some fruits and flavours will not go too well with some spirits, so make your choice carefully. I've yet to find any whisky infusions, simply because the whisky is the dominant flavour and it's far too strong. Can you imagine whisky and grapefruit or apricots? But vodka with kiwi, honey or lime is quite palatable. I have found that a lot of dried fruits work well in a spirit. You can use dried fruit in vodka, draw the flavour off it and when the drink has all gone use the fruit in a dessert, cake or a chutney. Why waste?

If you are making a brandy or vodka or gin, don't assume that all the same ingredients may be used willy-nilly. They can't, and a lot of either common sense or trial and error is involved. Lots of herbs will fit in well with a gin or vodka but wouldn't work with any other spirit. I've drawn up three vodka-based infusions for you to try. You might think one or two sound a bit strange, but I can tell you they are beautiful and will open your eyes to what you can achieve.

LAVENDER-INFUSED VODKA

Ingredients

¾ litre of vodka, doesn't have to be expensive
Two sprigs of lavender and one of rosemary

Method

Wash the herbs well, dry and place in an airtight jar. Add the vodka, shake well and store in a dark place for five days. Check it every day for flavour. Once it's at your taste level, remove the lavender and rosemary, and strain through a coffee filter to ensure there are no foreign bodies kicking around. Bottle and store as normal vodka.

GARLIC VODKA

Ingredients

1 medium-sized garlic bulb
2 sprigs of basil
¾ litre of your choice of vodka

Method

Split the bulb and remove the skins. Wash the basil. Add the garlic and basil to the vodka, shake well and leave for five days, testing each day for flavour. Decant into the original bottle.

MINT VODKA

Ingredients

¾ litre of vodka
1 clove
A small handful of mint leaves

Method

Follow the same method as for the previous infusions.

GIN INFUSIONS

Gin is another fine medium to use if you are thinking of an infusion and you can use a range of flavours or infusions with it. My friend Trevor has been known to go through the hedgerow like a demented terrier looking for things to eat, drink or make into clothes. Often he finds unmentionable things that he will use in all manner of ways. I've known Trevor find berries and leaves and take them off to his unkempt home and start making things. Sloe berries, cucumbers, wild strawberries, damsons and unripe nuts. One day he offered me a drink to try. I quivered, looking around his kitchen, with the numerous cats crawling all over his mountains of plates and groceries. He poured me an infused gin that smelt very light, citrus-like and clear. It was, or so I thought, lemon gin. Close but no cigar. It was gin but had been infused not by using a far from local lemon but with a very local lemon verbena. It was lovely, and well worth a try, though if you can't find verbena try lemon balm.

LEMON VERBENA GIN

The recipe for this infusion is very simple.

Ingredients

A litre of cheap gin
2 or 3 leaves of verbena balm or three large lemons
Around 200g sugar, use white granulated or caster as it will dissolve easily

Method

Remove around one fifth of the gin (about 200 ml). Don't drink it, but put it to one side – you are just making space in the bottle and will return this later. Rip the leaves up and place them in the bottle.

Add the sugar to the bottled gin and replace the 200 ml of gin back in the bottle. Give it a damn good shake. Leave it somewhere cool, dark and undisturbed by others. Give it a good shake occasionally. Leave it as long as you like to infuse, it will improve the longer you leave it. But do drink it, don't just look at it and smile (if you want to do that, get married . . .).

SLOE GIN/VODKA

This is really easy. Take about 500 g of sloes, prick them all over and place in the freezer to kid them that winter has arrived. Once they are frozen, remove from the freezer and place in a vessel/jug and pour whatever spirit you fancy over them and allow to infuse over a good fortnight. Remove, strain and separate and replace the liquid into an airtight bottle and leave to improve with age.

BRANDY INFUSIONS

This type of infusion isn't really any different from the ones we have spoken about earlier. The only difference is your choice of ingredients. The method is fairly similar and the medium is also, just a little darker. If you are clever and like a good infusion, it's best to work with the seasons. So, as an example, I would pick blackcurrants in May, cherries in August, use shop-bought apricots through the summer and then pick blackberries in the autumn. The recipe is fairly straightforward.

Ingredients

1 kg cherries
Half a litre of brandy
180 g sugar, again caster or granulated – don't use icing sugar as it will ball and form into pockets
A small handful of bitter almonds

Method

Have a selection of clean, dry and sterilised bottles ready. Cut the cherries in half, stone them and ensure there are no stalks. Push the cherries into the bottles and sprinkle with your sugar. When the bottles are just nearly full of cherries pour enough brandy over them to ensure that they are covered. Add the almonds. Seal the bottles, make sure they are airtight and leave them in a cool, dark place to rest. Under the stairs, in the attic, or next to your bed are usually good places. You can do a similar recipe with apricots and blackberries/ blackcurrants. But remember, especially with the blackberries, you should not just wash them you should soak them in a little salt water so as to remove any unwanted guests. It might be trendy to drink spirits with a wiggly worm in but I don't think you would want them in a blackberry brandy.

SAKE INFUSIONS

If you do want to go that little bit further and opt for the continental touch, look east for a peach, nectarine or apricot sake. It's dead easy to make and has a kick on it like a mule, but only if you leave it for a while. This is a quick and simple recipe.

Ingredients

A couple of ripe nectarines, peaches or a few ripe apricots
1 litre sake

Method

Stone and score the skin of the fruit, cut the fruit into pieces and cover with the sake. Give it a good shake and keep it in the fridge for at least 24 hours. Strain through a clean muslin bag and decant into a clean sterilised container. Keep the fruit to one side. Serve the drink in chilled glasses with some of the fruit pieces in the glass. Surprisingly, when you infuse sake it doesn't last too long afterwards. The fruit will only last around three days and the sake about five. Good excuse to drink it quickly then . . .

FOR THE TEETOTAL

I know these are not necessarily infusions in the true sense of the word but they are fun, and you may not want something that is alcoholic. During my time in Ireland we were always given either a pink or blue lemonade on hot summer days, so that was twice a year and on a Wednesday as summer is a limited quantity.

TRADITIONAL LEMONADE

Here is the recipe and method for traditional lemonade. For blue lemonade, substitute 125 g of bilberries/blueberries, mixed and blended, for the lemons. For pink lemonade, use the basic lemonade recipe but add 2 teaspoons of grenadine syrup.

Ingredients

2 lemons (preferably unwaxed)
700 ml water
125 g sugar

Method

Split the zest of one lemon into two heat-resistant jugs and pour 300 ml of boiling water into one of them. Leave it for an hour. Juice both lemons and add to the water. Meanwhile place your 125 g sugar into a pan, add 100 ml of water and gently heat until the sugar has gone. Pour this into a jug and leave to one side until it cools. Now pour the jug of zest water slowly through a sieve into the jug that has the other zest in it and discard the zest remaining in the sieve. Add the sugar water to the main mixture. Then add 300 ml of cold water and some ice and stir and serve to your guests with a smug smile.

CHAPTER 7

A TASTE OF THE MIDDLE EAST

Over the years I have learned a great deal about the beauty of the desert, the sand, the people, the ancient culture, and of course its food and drink. Arab hospitality is legendary and Bedouin food and drink under the stars with a warm, whipped wind is haunting. I spent some time in the desert plain in the Rub al Khali, or 'empty quarter', just a little west of Muscat, in Oman. We had climbed and four-tracked through the Jebal Akhtar all day in temperatures of 45°C. Now I know why the holiday was really cheap . . . Oman in August is empty through the day as it's too hot to move, and we were climbing, trekking and being mad Englishmen, merely missing the mad dogs.

Camping in the Rub al Khali under so many stars and hearing so many different sounds, imagine our surprise when we received visitors. 'Bonjour,' said this heavily accented Arab chappie. He spoke a little English but mainly communicated in French. He told us that we were fools camping in a wadi as it was going to rain and we were in danger of being washed away and never found. Being cautious European boys we smiled, looked at his rifle and his dagger and accepted his kind offer of dinner. We all feared we were going to be offered goat's eyes and other unmentionables. We got to his tent about three miles away, met his family and settled for some grub. He opened several tins of tuna for us, produced some Hellman's mayonnaise and bread; all very civilised. Then he whipped out some lemonade, but it was very different from any I had tried before. All I can describe it as is desert lemonade. His wife explained what it was, how it was made and the ingredients. It was essentially three lemons, three limes, a cup of granulated sugar, 1 teaspoon of orange blossom water, a small handful of fresh mint and a litre of water. My friend Charlie asked was there any ice. Fool!

You essentially blend the water, orange blossom water, citrus juices and mint together. Shake and chill best you can. It was very nice, not sweet or fizzy. If you like it sweeter just add more sugar.

THIS DESERT LIFE

There we were, living like Arabs under the stars until my friend Christoph took a shine to one of this chap's daughters. They started the giggly, smiley exchange of glances and that was it. We had abused his hospitality, so he promptly told us to clear off and get out. Off we went, only for Charlie to stick his head through the tent flap and ask which way our camp was. My French was fairly basic then, but even I knew what 'sod off' was. We stumbled around the desert telling each other stories of desert-dwelling creatures that would eat you alive, or scorpions that would crawl up your leg and nibble your nuts. I had this vision that we should stop where we were for fear of walking around the desert for hours in circles, missing our camp and dying a dreadfully slow death. So we stopped, in perfect silence now, a chill wind blowing, no warm drinks and no warm clothes. But there we stayed for the rest of the night. We awoke in the morning stiff and cold. Charlie had a frost on him where the sweat of his body had frozen; he was actually in a bad way. When we lifted our heads up we were amazed to find the camp – our camp, with its hot tea and warm sleeping bags and numerous tog fleeces – was about 200 yards away. How I love the desert and her people.

CHAPTER 8

MAKING PERRY

Perry is a brew similar to cider, but it's made from pears – not just any old pears but perry pears. Perry is traditionally made in the three counties of Gloucestershire, Worcestershire and Herefordshire, although you do find that perry is also made in France (in Normandy and Anjou, where it is called *poire*) and follows a similar process. It's hard to say whether it came from France first and crossed over to England, or vice versa. Perry is also found in South Wales. Of all the drinks I make I am a real fan of mead, but with all honesty I am an even bigger fan of perry. It's so crisp and light, with a beautiful sparkle of bubbles on your tongue, and also with a slightly perfumed flavour.

So, how is perry made? Well, as with any process you need to start at the beginning, with picking your fruit. The same rules apply to pears as to apples: windfalls are fine, but don't use heavily bruised ones as you will need to leave them for two to three days to a week to mature. If you use pears straight off the bough they will have little natural sugar in them. So, a few days to rest and mature will only serve to help them and your brew. I've never seen Hawky as excited about a product as he gets about perry. So watching and helping him that first time was a magical experience. I did ask him once about leaving the pears for a longer time. His view was that this was pointless as the pears will rot from the inside out. While you might think that you have nice sweet pear flesh, in fact what you have is rotting and will produce a cloudy brew with the fermentation process all over the place – ultimately your perry will spoil and be undrinkable. Tragic.

When your pears are ripe and are full of sweet bountifulness, crush them using the same process as for apples in the cider-making process. However, unlike the cider spoken about earlier, the pulp or pomace that you create out of the pears is left to stand for a period before being pressed. This allows the tannins to be discharged so that that when finished it will be a cloudy brew like a cloudy cider or wheat beer. You leave the pomace to stand for around 24 hours or certainly overnight if you can't wait, then crush it using a cider press.

The pressed juice is fermented just as for cider and is matured in storage tanks. A traditional perry is served flat and cloudy. Some mass-produced ones don't have that cloudiness and therefore some people think when making a cloudy perry that they've done it all wrong.

PEAR TYPES

The quality of your brew will depend on what type of pears you use. Just as with apples and honey, there are different types, flavours, abundance, etc. Pears come in a number of categories: sweet, medium, bittersweet, bittersharp.

Sweet pears

A sweet pear like a **Williams** is ideal for cider, as it's sweet and juicy with a distinct pear drop flavour when it's fully ripe. (If you are not of a certain age, you may not know what pear drops are: they are hard sugar sweets with a slightly artificial flavour, although the mighty Williams is far from artificial.) The **Rocha** is an equal match to the **Williams**. Originally from Portugal it is small, pale and green/yellow in colour, whilst being beautiful in flavour. Sweet pears have a fairly low acidity level, around about 0.2% per volume, coupled with fairly low tannin content. If you are looking for ultra-sweet you might want to fiddle with the **Comice** pear. This is a plump pear with a green to rustic brown flesh and a very sweet buttery taste.

Medium pears

Medium sharp flavours can be found in the **Concorde** variety, which is a hybrid of the **Comice** and the **Conference**. As a variety, it is very new, originating as recently as 1977. It grows in a similar way to the **Conference** but is more russet. This variety, depending on the lateness of the season, can produce a sweet and medium pear that will affect your initial brew. The **Packham**, an Australian pear, is good as a medium but equally as good as a pear for combining flavours. It can be a rich, cream pear and, if picked early, it can have a medium to sweet flavour. This category generally has an acidity of between 0.2 and 0.6% and a low tannin content.

Bittersweet pears

Bittersweet pears are few and far between and few fall this way. However, you can engineer a bitter sweet experience by using immature pears, mainly conference ones. These pears have an acidity of above 0.45% and a very low tannin content.

Bittersharp pears

These pears have an acidity of 0.45% and a tannin content as low as 0.2%. You should find that these pears have a penetrating flavour. Although it is classed as bittersharp, the flavour is not really a sharp, more a striking flavour. When you use these pears you can take comfort that they are not for eating, they are the crab apples of the pear world. Try looking for a **Red Pear** or a **Yellow Huffcap**.

GOLDEN PERRY

This is a wonderfully dry, crisp pear cider. In fact, it's not too far removed from a good white wine – the only indication that it's not is the pear flavour and aroma. To get to this stage of superb perry you will need to add the following:

Ingredients

1.5 teaspoons citric acid
0.9 kg soft light brown sugar
5 teaspoons malic acid
18 litres squeezed pears
1.8 kg white sugar
3 teaspoons tartaric acid
1 teaspoon tannin
2 teaspoons acid blend
10 g champagne yeast

Method

Always make sure everything is sparklingly clean and free from anything nasty and germ-like. Warm 3.7 litres of the pear juice and dissolve the sugars in it along with the rest of the ingredients. Give it a really good stir to ensure everything is combined and dissolved. Next take a cup of warm water at no more than 37°C and dissolve your yeast in it. When the sugars are dissolved, combine the remaining pear juice and mixture into a large five-gallon carboy. Don't forget to fit your blow-off valve and pitch the yeast. As the mix starts to gurgle and ferment keep an eye on the levels and top up with pear juice if need be. After a month the fermentation process will start to slow down and, when it does, transfer or rack to a second carboy and top up again. After about 45 days you should be able to bottle it. Personally I would leave it a bit longer but if you are desperate to try it, give it until around the 45-day mark. Six months is the best time to crack open a bottle as it will have matured to very best level.

CHAPTER 9

MAKING MEAD

Mead isn't just about honey and the magic of alchemy. Mead has developed all over the world at almost the same time, from Ethiopia to Scandinavia, Poland and Russia, where it's called Sbiten. In Finland, sweet mead called Sima is a seasonal brew associated with May Day festivals. It's spiced and pulped unlike the Ethiopian varieties. Ethiopian mead is known as Tej. During the second fermentation period raisins are added to control the amount of sugars. The raisins also act as an indicator of readiness for consumption as they will rise to the top when it's time to drink it. In South Africa, Mead is known by the Xhosa people as iQhilika.

Mead can be altered from its original state by the inclusion of tea leaves – and as you might expect, each different type of tea leaf makes a different type of mead. You can also vary your mead by using different types of honey. I would always start off by using a cheap

Chinese honey that you can get for buttons from any supermarket. Make your mistakes with this, but then try experimenting with Mexican Yucatan, Ethiopian highland, Tasmanian leatherwood or a Scottish heather variety. You can even add cherries in your mead mix, or apples or grain. This is usually referred to as melomel. Some cultures have always used a variety of berry juices and spices like a mulled wine, or even herbs.

At Hawky's house one day he offered me a mead tasting session. With a scuttle and a scurry like a deranged terrier, he went off to find a selection of meads. Different bottles of differing ages appeared, all with a different story. Out came a number of glasses and samples were poured. The first one I tasted was the essence of cat's pee, or as my friends in Provence call it, *pipi de chat.* The last was a ten-year-old beauty, smooth, clear, crisp with a hint of honey. Like a fine wine coupled with an aged single malt, it was indeed the drink of the Gods.

THE BASIC RECIPE

Now what I am going to tell you cannot be repeated, and this book will self-destruct in five seconds . . . This is an age old recipe, and all you need for the basics are 1 packet of champagne yeast, 1 teaspoon of yeast nutrient, 1 teaspoon of acid blend, 1.5 kg of honey (your choice), 5 litres of unchlorinated water. (That is, don't use chlorinated tap water. Originally you were instructed to take rain water, but I wouldn't chance it these days. You're better off with boiled water that has been allowed to cool, or use spring water if you can.) And that's all there is to it, except time. As I said above, when you are starting off, use the cheapest materials possible. Don't go out and buy heather or manuka honey because it's the best, buy some cheap, supermarket own brand. The difference in cost is vast. At the time of writing, low cost honey sells for around 69p for 340 g, manuka or other good honey will cost up to £75 a kilo. You will learn from your mistakes over time and move on to the more expensive stuff to improve your brew. One honey that is superb for brewing with is a dark rich, almost molasses like, sycamore honey.

THE BASIC METHOD

The process is actually quite an easy one. You need a sterilised container, just like the one used for making cider, and if you are using a liquid yeast mix, make it in advance.

Step one

Measure your water to fill your demijohn, which will usually be 3.3 litres. Then return the water to a stainless steel brewing pot. Bring this water to a good strong rolling boil and stir in the honey. Take care to add it in slowly so that it dissolves, otherwise it will collect as a cooked lump at the bottom of the pan. Then add the acid blend. Make sure the contents don't boil over, because you will find a sticky mess forever and when it comes to your calculations you will be thrown out with incorrect amounts.

Step two

Cover your pan with some clean foil and allow it to cool naturally to around 37°C. Don't try and force it to cool, but as long as it's covered you could leave it outside or place a large spoon upside down underneath the pan to allow cool air to flow under the base of the pan. Pour in the honey/yeast mix and stir in your yeast starter and allow to dissolve. Transfer to the demijohn and add the bung and a fermentation lock. Put the demijohn to one side and clean up the mess before your wife comes home. If within 24 hours your demijohn isn't bubbling rapidly and there isn't a foam starting, then your mead isn't mead, its mud. Place in a cool dark place (I always use my wife's purse as it's never opened, and it's very deep and hides a lot of secrets). Check it daily. If all goes well, a thick sediment will build up on the bottom of the demijohn. When the sediment has reached around 2–3 cm depth, the mead will need racking. To prevent the sediment passing to your next vessel you will need to syphon the contents between each demijohn. As you start to syphon off the mix, ensure that you control the depth of the tube and that it doesn't enter into the sediment. If it does, you will need to start again once the sediment has settled. As you do your racking, try to disturb the mead as little as possible.

Step three

When you have completed the racking process, top up the demijohn with fresh water. Sterilise a bung and plug the neck of the demijohn, and don't forget to add a fermentation lock. As the fermentation process slows down your mead should be exposed to as little oxygen as possible. Check your brew on a daily basis, so much so that it should be sufficient to upset your wife. Look at the brew with the look a father gives to his newborn and say things like, 'Isn't she beautiful!', 'Look at that!', and 'Well I never.' That should upset her sufficiently . . . If a new level of sediment builds up on the original, re-rack it. If the water level falls below the bung, top it up with fresh water. If after a couple of weeks the bubbles disappear, then the fermentation process is over, but don't be too impatient as the whole process can take between two and six months.

Bottling

At this stage you should bottle your mead and let it age like a good whisky. You will be best to bottle your mead in bottles with a clasp cap. The ones that Grolsch comes in are the best sort to use as the contents tend to become somewhat active. You can use screw tops or white wine bottles but they must have new clean corks.

BRAGGOT (IT'S MEAD, JIM, BUT NOT AS WE KNOW IT)

Braggot (also known as bracket, or brackett) is a wonderful drink. It's also called ale mead in some parts of the country but appears to have its origins in medieval Wales/England and is still popular around the Welsh Marches and Offa's Dyke area. It is known as Bragawd in Welsh and this appears to have influenced the English variation of the name.

It is considered to be more of an ale than a mead because it is a mixture of honey with hops and latterly with malt, with or without the addition of hops. It is made in the same way as ale but with the inclusion of honey at the stage where you normally add the finishing hops. If you are using 2 lb of malt extract you must use 2 lb of wild flower honey. Go for one that is quite runny but not so fast that you have to chase it.

A basic braggot recipe

Braggot is a rather odd brew as it comes in either weak or strong format. It uses some of the ingredients of mead and some of ale. The basic recipe is thus:

Ingredients

2 kg wild flower honey
2 sliced lemons
30 g cascading finishing hops
30 Fuggles finishing yeast
1.5 kg malt extract
5 litres water – which must be unchlorinated

Method

Now making this is a piece of cake. You follow the basic mead recipe detailed earlier on and at the boiling stage add the finishing hops. Take the big pot off the heat and remove the hops after five minutes. Add the sliced lemons – always go for unwaxed lemons if you can but at the very least fresh ones; don't ever be tempted to cut corners and use the bottled stuff. You should leave the lemons having a bath for around half an hour until their skins have gone all smooth like a human's, not wrinkly like a lemon (only kidding, just leave them for 30 minutes and then remove them). Pass the liquid through a sieve just to make sure that no lemony bits have been left behind in your brew. Allow the liquor to cool and proceed as the usual method describes. You must leave the braggot to mature for around a year once you've bottled it. You should then have a good strong brew to be proud of – but if you want a weaker brew you can leave it just for a month or two.

BLACK MEAD

I was once given black mead on an island named Krk (took me an age to figure out how to pronounce that). The island is off the Dalmatian coast and connected by a rather worrying looking bridge. After settling into our rooms we were presented with a drink of plum brandy that tasted so rough the enamel on my teeth disappeared almost instantaneously. The landlord could see I was a bit of a pathetic sort and offered me some black mead. I explained in my best pidgin English and hand movements that I was a beekeeper. He explained about the bees and the mead in his best pidgin Serbo-Croat. Now that was difficult to understand, but trying to get the recipe was tantamount to near impossible.

So he made a batch for me and I watched patiently. The only added difference was the inclusion of some locally-picked blackcurrants and a few hazelnuts. I have made this since and when the blackcurrants have all gone, blackberries are just as good. You must though pass your brew through a fine sieve to collect any stray seeds and bugs. This inclusion makes a dark, warm almost glowing mead with a flavour reminiscent of liquorice, perfect at room temperature in the winter, or chilled and served on the terrace in summer. If you don't have a terrace, try a backyard; it works just as well.

MELOMEL

In Spain I was given mead that was to influence the way I made my mead in the future. No longer was I just a honey, yeast and water man. I went to see my friend Gillian in Ronda, up in the hills and miles from the tourists and the kiss-me-quick hats. She took me to a friend of hers who kept bees and made a fruit mead called melomel. This simple inclusion of fruit, either singularly or mixed, changed my favourite tipple into a regular occasion. I would have it on cornflakes, brush my teeth with it and wash my hair in it. Well I felt I could – I certainly wanted to. Gillian's friend explained that he would only ever use what was local to him, but being where he was he had almost the contents of my local supermarket's fruit and veg counter on his doorstep. He showed me a mead with a variety of nuts in it that gave it a dry taste, almost edgy (it certainly set my teeth on edge). He also showed me some of his mead that he had laid down like a good wine or whisky. He gave me a shot and it felt just like being given a spirit not a wine. It was just like a single malt or a smooth cognac, and had been lying down for around eight years.

Mead with melon in is delicious. But (surprisingly) only honeydew melons will work for this – do not use watermelons as they are too watery, and don't be tempted by the cantaloupe melon as they make your mead taste and smell like nail polish remover. (Gillian's friend said this with a shake of his head and a grimace that appeared across the full width of his face.) I think it's fair to say that my favourite has to be the strawberry/raspberry mix and the peach/nectarine duo. Both were beautiful. What I was fascinated by the most was the almost infinite combinations of fruit and/or nuts that could be added to the mead. I did ask him about adding vegetables to the mead, and he almost killed me with his death ray glare. But I am thinking, come the autumn and the revolution I might try fiddling with a few parsnips and add them to my mead. I do think peas (crushed) and/or pea pods would work well. Tomatoes could work well also. I'm also wondering about using the likes of nasturtiums and dandelions, perhaps nettles – there's so much open to the adventurous mead maker. Another of my favourites is metheglin, a spiced variety of mead, found in a number of places, and I've wondered for a long time whether you could make a combination of melomel and metheglin, a spiced or cinnamon-flavoured nectarine mead.

CYSER

Cyser is a fermented apple juice and diluted honey. It may well be a development of cider. The two products do work well together. You can use any apple juice, it doesn't have to be freshly pressed and from your own trees. Obviously it's nice if you can use your own, but any old apple juice from the supermarket works very well. Ferment your apple juice in the usual manner and add some diluted wild flower honey.

OXYMEL

You can get a mead made with wine vinegar, called Oxymel. Tastes great, but it sounds like a spot cream for teenagers.

PYMENT

Pyment is a blend of red and/or white or both grapes. It's sometimes called white mead or pink mead.

RHODOMEL

I was sent a sample of this by a chap in France who was looking to sell it in England. This is mead that has the inclusion of rosehips, rose petals and rose water. I can't see why he needed a distributor in the UK as the product sold itself. You make it in the same way as the other meads.

SACK MEAD

I was once given sack mead in New Zealand. I was worried that this would be some odd brew, which had been strained through a sack that had once contained a dead badger. Much to my surprise, there aren't any badgers in New Zealand. The whole process of making sack mead was the same as let's say 'normal' mead, other than that the brewers had doubled and sometimes trebled the amount of honey.

For those of you not so well versed in making mead you might think this was a cunning plan to make it a lot sweeter, in fact it didn't work that way at all. What it did produce, after laying down for a while, was what I can only describe as a very nice single malt. Or even a slightly golden very precise sake. It was a beautiful experience, blue sky, fluffy white clouds, rolling hills and worried sheep. I sat there on a veranda, sipping away at my new-found friend whilst my other new-found friend poured me another.

The new-found friend in question was called Bernard Mathews, which I found really funny. Every time he introduced himself I would laugh, and the more mead I drank the more I would giggle. I explained but it lost itself in translation. 'Hello, I'm Bernard Mathews.'

SHORT MEAD

Bernie gave me some of another brew he had made, a mead-based brew called short mead. It was a quick version and tasted less of nectar and more of the sack that had had the badger in. In essence, you didn't leave the mead to mature as long and almost drank it at the shortest possible available time. It was raw, like a Beaujolais nouveau, not strong in alcohol, and definitely not as pleasant as the previous brew. You just drank it quickly.

SHOW MEAD

From the back of his 'man cave', Bernie produced a nice mead he referred to as a 'show mead'. A simple no-nonsense, plain mead, that was the basic recipe. It had no fruits, nuts, extra sugar or spices in it and after the two others it was nice to return to Planet Craig and be able to see I had retained all my fingers and toes. 'Hello I'm Bernard Mathews!' A classic.

OAK LEAF MELOMEL MEAD

One afternoon in late September/early October many years ago, my dear old father and I were abroad when we passed an old oak tree. He stretched over a ditch and started to pick the dry brown withered leaves from about chest height. I watched and didn't question. Stuffing the pockets of his battered jacket he soon found that they were full, so off came his cap and he began to stuff the leaves into that as well. Once he had enough we went on our way, him smiling, me still not questioning him. When we arrived home he took the leaves out of his clothing and set about getting settled for the evening.

The next day he decided to explain to me what the oak leaves were for. To my surprise he was making mead, or to give it its full name, oak leaf melomel mead. As I said earlier on he would always want anything for free, and taking from nature was right up his street. Admittedly, he always thanked the tree, plant, hive etc. for the gift. He always respected nature and thanked it.

Every answer is in nature, he used to say. So he set about making this mix that I had never seen him make before. You have to bear in mind that my father never worked in imperial measures, let alone metric – his recipes were usually about a cap full of leaves and a handful of this. So here is the oak leaf melomel recipe:

Ingredients

4 kg loose, runny honey
5 litres unchlorinated water

500 g chopped plump raisins (you might want to soak these in cold tea overnight to get that really fat plumpness going)
One cap full and two pockets full of dry, brown withered oak leaves (don't use green leaves, as they can be poisonous)
1 large piece of bruised ginger (you can beat the ginger up yourself – just make sure the skin and flesh are pliable) that with some effort you could break it in half
Yeast and about 6 teaspoons of yeast nutrient

Method

Pour the 5 litres of boiling water over the oak leaves in a fermenting bucket. Cover the bucket with a lid, cloth or tinfoil or cling film and leave it to infuse for around four to five days. At the end of this time strain them through a muslin bag and into a large, heavy-bottomed pan. Place your pan on a low heat, then add the ginger and raisins to the oak leaf liquor and add the honey, just a little at a time. I would say add it in a constant dribble, slow running, allowing the honey to dissolve as it runs in. You don't want it to clump together in a mess. At this stage add the yeast and the yeast nutrients, to kick-start the fermentation process off. If you can do this in a thoroughly filthy kitchen, with a cat that sleeps on the ingredients, you will obtain the original Irish flavour that my father's father used to produce. Now take the mix off the heat, remove the ginger and leave it to cool. From this stage on you can return to following the basic mead recipe and enjoy your mead. A word of warning! Please allow this creation of God's to mature for at least a year once you've bottled it. If you prefer a drier mead ease back on the honey, and do the opposite if you like it sweeter.

NETTLE MEAD

My father was one of those immigrants who swayed between the 'old country' and the place he called home. Everything was better in the old country, but he grew to love England and when he returned to Ireland couldn't find what he was looking for. The things he brought with him were not materialistic possessions but the stories, recipes and country practices that he passed on to me. I asked him about his mead and alcohol infused recipes and he told me of a very interesting one. It's a variation on the oak leaf mead. Surprisingly, it didn't involve potatoes but did involve nettles. In the spring one year we picked the youngest, sweetest nettles – just those above about a foot high and way above the height of a dog's peeing aim. It was like tea picking, selecting only the youngest and the greenest shoots and leaves. My father (in typical Irish storyteller fashion, with a mix of Blarney, fact and embroidery) told me this recipe was thousands of years old, which I believed until I saw the ingredients . . .

For nettle mead you will need rubber gloves, sharp scissors and some sting cream as one will always get you. This mead is bright green, as you might have guessed. The reason why I have said you need to pick nice spring nettles is because as they get older they taste a little woody and a tad earthy. Old nettles won't add to the flavour and the colour won't be there either. This is the Irish in me coming out. You can do a lot with nettles, cheese, soup, pâté and bread . . . loads. Here's the recipe for nettle mead.

Ingredients

2 litres young spring green nettle leaves (if you're not sure what this looks like, try one plastic supermarket shopping bag full)
4 litres water
3 oranges, segmented, including the peel and pips

3 lemons, as for the oranges
2 kg runny honey
2 quartered nutmegs
360 g bruised fresh ginger
6 tablespoons allspice berries
240 g hops
15 g yeast
Two pieces of toast!!
(You can see why I eventually realised my father was kidding when he said this recipe was thousands of years old. It was the inclusion of the citrus fruits that got me. He had a good soul though . . .)

Method

Mix the nettles, the water and the citrus fruits together in a large pan. Bring it to a boil and allow to boil gently, not a simmer but a slow boil, for at least 40 minutes. Remove from the heat and strain the mix through a muslin bag. Once strained return the liquor to the heat and allow to boil. (I had a boil once. Dreadful!) Add your honey slowly and allow this to dissolve. Boil for an hour and skim any crap off the surface: lots of scum will rise and you will need to remove it straight away otherwise you will have a very cloudy brew. Add the spices and hops and boil for at least another ten minutes.

Again strain your liquor through the muslin bag and into a fermentation bucket. Cover and allow to cool to a lukewarm temperature. Now spread a piece of toast with the 15 g of yeast and float it out on the surface of the brew. Butter the other piece of toast and eat it whilst you wait for the first slice to get cracking. Leave toast one for three days and allow the brew to ferment. Then skim the surface and transfer the brew to a fermenting bottle, which must have an airlock. After about a fortnight, fermentation should have stopped and no more bubbles will be seen. You should at this stage rack the bottles. Always use a good strong stopper to seal them and lay down in a dark cool place. Within about three to six months your bottles of green fun will be ready. Why not try to have them ready for St Patrick's Day, 17 March?

FRUIT MEAD

One recipe that wasn't given to me by my father was one using fruits in mead, either whole, preserved, or as a part of the actual brew. At different times of the year you may well find yourself in the most fortunate of times when fruits become available. In early summer you may have an abundance of soft fruits such as raspberries, strawberries and tayberries etc., and in some cases the same in late summer. Throughout the summer there are lots of the softer tree and ground fruits, such as plums, bilberries etc., and in the larger supermarkets that import fruit all year round, sometimes they have some fruit going cheap that haven't gone down too well with their customers but will make delicious mead, things like Sharon fruit, or kiwi. In the autumn, there is an abundance of hedgerow fruits available, like blackberries and wild strawberries. I was told that hawthorn berries, if boiled, are fine but do not give a particularly good taste. (So really, why would you bother then?) I have also heard about people drawing off the syrup from rose hips and using it to replace some of the honey content. I've never tried it but it sounds nice. If you do fancy messing around with other materials try looking at using plums or raspberries as either make a nice delicate rose type of mead. Here's a basic fruit mead recipe:

Ingredients

1 kg soft fruit, washed (e.g. plums, stoned; strawberries, cored and stalked)

1 cinnamon stick about 5 inches long
2.5 litres water
Yeast and yeast nutrients
14 kg runny honey
1 unwaxed lemon
1 crushed Campden tablet

Method

Soak your fruits in the crushed Campden tablet and cold water for around an hour to kill off any natural yeasts. I know that sounds a little silly, killing off the natural yeast, but as you can't measure the natural you can't control it. Anyway, boil your water and add the honey slowly, allowing it to dissolve thoroughly. Once you get to boiling point, leave it to bubble away for about ten minutes and then reduce it to a gentle ticking over simmer. Add your prepared fruits, but don't include any bruised or damaged ones. Allow your brew to cool to room temperature, add your fruit and a quartered lemon and don't forget the cinnamon stick. Activate your yeast, add to the mix and add your yeast nutrient. You are probably seeing a trend here. Move your liquor to the fermentation bin and stand it in a warm place for a few days; an airing cupboard is a good place. Give it a stir daily. When the rapid, violent fermentation period has come to an end, strain the liquor through a muslin bag and straight into a demijohn. You need to squeeze the cooked fruits to extract any further juice. (Don't be too enthusiastic with this though, as you might make the brew cloudy – as you won't be able to extract the seeds from a strawberry you will find that there will be seeds in your strawberry mead. You might get them out with a muslin bag but don't be surprised if some make it through.) Fit your lock and leave again in a warm place to ferment. Once a couple of weeks have passed, rack the brew into a clean demijohn and monitor the level of gravity until the mead clears. Don't be kidded that the fermentation process has stopped. I've known mead to stop, start and stop all over again. The best way to decide when it has truly stopped is to keep a written record and if after three days it's not showing any signs of fermenting, it's fine. Settle in bottles and leave for three to six months. And enjoy.

CHAPTER 10

MAKING BEER

We do know that beer has been brewed from the dawn of time. No one is quite sure exactly what went into the first beers and they may very well have been made from apples or a collection of things. I once used to prison visit a friend from university who had fallen by the wayside and had so many credit cards in other folk's names that he was eventually caught and incarcerated. On one visit my friend told me of the things he missed. The usual things were mentioned – liberty, privacy and an American Express Gold card, as you might expect. I asked him about his omission of beer and/or alcohol (as my friend and I had been good customers of the Eldon Arms in Preston); he told me there was a generous supply of alcohol in prison and that I need not worry.

He further told me how it was made. This point worried me . . . All you needed, he said, was old bread, orange juice and spit. This took me by surprise. He told me of the fermentation process, the actions of bacteria and sugar; all sounded fascinating, until he told me that if you want to do it in a decent batch you needed to mix yours with everybody else's. He smiled and told me that the orange juice for breakfast and the container it came in were ideal, especially for moving consignments of 'mixture' around the prison in. And it knocked me for six. Yet why should this be any different from our 'ideal' caveman and his early experiments with brewing? It has been argued that it was alcohol and brewing, that were the catalyst for the hunter-gatherers to settle down. Waiting for your precious brew to come to fruition is probably good enough reason to stay put. Cereals have certainly been one of the key factors for the settlement of mankind, and perhaps not just for the benefit they bring in terms of staple foods, but I don't know if I would ever be drawn to getting drunk at the expense of hepatitis, gingivitis or HIV like my friend in prison.

BREWING YOUR OWN: REASONS TO BE CHEERFUL

When you choose to brew your own you will find that there are a multitude of beers and a multitude of additions for you to choose from. You will also find that your brew will be dramatically different from the factory-produced beer. I suppose one of the reasons I would always give when asked why I would want to brew my own, is simply that it tastes better. I know I could wander to the pub and have a pint of consistent fizziness but if you brew your own, with the same ingredients, the same mix, and the same additions, the brew will always taste different. And this can be for a variety of factors, but doesn't include your next-door neighbour spitting in it. Brewing your own will be an awful lot cheaper than buying it, but it definitely won't be lacking in quality.

It's quite a challenge making your own anything. Making brews from kits is really easy and sometimes a really good starting point as once you have made something you enjoy, you will feel confident enough to start fiddling around, tweaking etc. and making your own 'special brew'. You will be able to make the brews that you want to drink. Pubs and off licences will offer you a limited amount of selection depending on who owns them and who supplies them. I went through a period of liking fruit beers from Belgium and Holland and wheat beers from Germany and Austria, yet I really struggled to get hold of them. It was then that the penny dropped: make your own, young man, make your own! And so I did. I've never looked back. Nor has my liver.

I found that I could experiment with a number of brews, get my friends round and taste test. We would do a blindfold test and mark each beer on fizz, taste, additions, gravity and personal taste. Great fun. But we were then able to produce a beer to our own personal taste. Most importantly you will be able to make beers or whatever you fancy, to your own strength. Although strength is a personal preference, this is usually the reason why a lot of people go for personal brewing, because they want it to be a personal product and therefore decide on their own colour, taste and most of all, strength.

A CAUTIONARY TALE

This story concerns two of my friends, who, for the sake of their anonymity, I will call Trevor and Anne. Their real names are Trevor and Anne. Trevor's brother died and he and Anne went to South Wales to sort out the cottage. Anne being a typical Yorkshire woman and not wanting to part with owt decided to keep many things. One box she found contained a goodly supply of brewing materials, demijohns, traps etc. so, being the good Yorkist she is, carried on looking for other brewing materials and stumbled upon several 1970s brewing kits. 'Make your own Party 7', the label cried out. So after looking for a sell by/use by date, she decided as there wasn't one it must be fit for use. I visited Trevor one winter's morning and he had made vast amounts of bubbling brown beer. He told me he had used the Party 7 mixes and had included a variety of additions like honey, elderflower and hazelnuts. Trevor thought they all tasted great. Personally, I thought they all tasted foul, mainly because it was 8 o'clock in the morning. So a bacon butty or so later, we tucked into our taste testing and by 10am were well and truly sloshed. I thought the one with the addition of honey tasted the best. They were all fine and had managed the last few decades admirably and produced a fine if not gassy brew. I had not seen Trevor as happy for years, as he worked his way through his brew collection. In the end, he missed out on most of November 1998, as the beer kit was out of date by then. Anne on the other hand regretted her find as her better half was good for nothing until about midwinter solstice. And the moral of this story is: beer lasts well if kept in the right conditions.

WHAT'S IT GOING TO BE, THEN? KIT OR MASH?

The ideal for beer making is something that is easy, tasty, not that messy that your wife will hit the roof, and something that will give you great pleasure in completing – and then explaining to your wife that you have saved so much money by not going to the pub. Well, what's it going to be, a kit or a mash?

The basic method for mashing is for you to soak ground malted barley in hot water and this produces a sweet wort. Sweet wort is then mixed with hops and this in turn produces hopped wort. You will then add yeast to the hopped wort mixture and leave it to ferment. As the beer matures in the bottles, sugar or carbon dioxide can be added for carbonation. That's it basically . . . But let's have a look at the processes in a bit more detail.

BREWING FROM A KIT

Three cheers for this process, as it is idiot proof. This is the easiest way of brewing and probably the safest. If you feel that this way is difficult, unsatisfying or not what you imagined, perhaps brewing isn't for you. You can buy a kit from a number of places, ranging from the likes of Boots the Chemist to a home-brew shop (of which there are many good ones online). These kits are in essence concentrated hopped worts, so steps one and two of the mashing process are already completed for you. The nice thing about these kits is that they concentrate the taste and flavour for you. When the hops are added to the wort, some of the excess liquid is purposefully evaporated under vacuum at a low temperature, to secure those delicate flavours, then the concentrate is pasteurised and placed in a tin. Voilà! All you need to do when you get your tin home is to reconstitute the concentrated wort back to its original density, ferment and then bottle. Very, very easy. Adding additionals to it, though, may disrupt the outcome. You may want to become a little more disciplined before you take that leap. You might want to throw some hops in just to add a little of the flavour that might have been lost in the vacuuming process. You may also find that the cheapest kit is not necessarily the best to buy. Cheap kits are fine but generally need an awful lot of sugar to kick start them. Remember, too, that the cheap kits won't produce a beer that is as flavoursome as you might have imagined.

USING A MALT EXTRACT

When you look at this method you may feel it is too complex but in reality it isn't and is nothing to be afraid of. In this process the malt extract does not contain hops and when you dilute and heat the malt extract it gives you the equivalent of a sweet wort. You obtain the hop flavour by adding a muslin bag full of hops, sometimes known as a sparge bag (I prefer the name sparge, as it always sounds vaguely rude to me). The sparge bag should be added for around 20 minutes towards the end of the heating process. The end product is hopped wort and should be fermented and bottled.

BREWING WITH A HALF OR PARTIAL MASH

The half mash is a halfway version of a full mash that incorporates a half mash and the concentrate from a malt kit. The sweet wort is made from a combination of speciality grains that are soaked in hot water and malt extract. I suppose the advantages of a partial mash over a full one are that you don't require too much space, equipment or skills to produce it all in. And the advantages of partial over full malt extract brew are that you have the final say over the brew and much more control. This is a real advantage when you are starting out as you feel that you have at least mastered one side of the brewing process and can move on to other more complicated ones.

BREWING WITH FULL MASH: KEEP CALM AND CARRY ON

You have to accept that sometimes things are easy in life, and sometimes they are more difficult. And this is the *pièce de résistance.* It is because of this that you shouldn't really attempt this manoeuvre first. The full mash does require an element of skill and effort. It is only when you have obtained these skills that I would advise you to attempt this. This is the stage that will reward you with the choice of additions to your beer, offer you a different taste or gravity.

To produce a full-on mash you will need a grist. Now this consists of crushed dry grains that are mixed before mashing. More often the majority of this type of grist would be a pale malt with a small amount of crystal malt added. You can use other grains such as wheat, dark roasted malts and maize to obtain a different flavour and colour.

Your grist is mashed (soaked in hot water for a couple of hours). This process converts the starch found in the grist into sugar. The mash is then, yes you guessed it, 'sparged'. You rinse the sparge bag and contents with water to remove as much sugar from the grain as possible. Once this process has been completed the hops are added (to the wort) and then the hopped wort is boiled for around an hour. It is this heating stage that brings out the flavour from the hops and helps to sterilise, whilst at the same time it cleans the protein debris from the wort. Sounds very technical but don't be worried by it. What's the worst you can do? Kill someone?

The wort is then left to cool to the appropriate temperature (about 65°F, or 18°C) so that the yeast can then be added. Your brew will then need around 10 to 14 days to ferment. After fermentation has passed, the brew should be bottled, kegged and a small amount of sugar should be added to kick start a secondary fermentation. This is to provide enough carbon dioxide gas to provide the beer with a head.

KEEPING EVERYTHING CLEAN

If you are to do this properly and not make any mistakes you really need to have cleaned your surfaces well. Any surface that the beer comes into contact with will need to be as clean as a dentist's tool. Any residue, whether it's old cleaning products that have dried, or the tiniest amount of grease, will all need removed, and all surfaces will have to be cleaned till spotless. If you do have foreign bodies, no matter how small, they might well have contaminants in them and easily allow bacteria to multiply. In this case it would be the wrong sort of bacteria multiplying and their presence will spoil your hard work.

You must remove all evidence of anything that you know or consider might be a contaminant. Only use a scentless washing-up liquid, use plenty of hot water and rinse in cool water. Remember the golden rule: loose lips sink ships. This won't help you at all but will make you giggle every time you hear it.

Sanitising, or sterilising (which is the same thing), will reduce any nasties to a harmless level. I find that, if you borrow materials to use, sometimes they are rusted – if that's the case, don't bother sanitising them, just give them back as sanitising won't prevent chemical poisoning. After you have cleaned all your equipment and surfaces, you must also sanitise whatever comes into contact with the beer after it has been boiled. Remember though, you don't actually have to sanitise the equipment that comes into contact with your wort before and during the boil, as the boiling process will sterilise both the beer and pot.

CLEANLINESS FOR BOTTLING OR KEGGING

When you are transferring beer to whatever container it must be done smoothly and quickly.

Make sure everything is clean, and if you do choose to use a bleach compound for cleaning, make sure it is an unscented bleach, otherwise everything will smell like a freshly-scrubbed bog. You need to use this as a diluted solution: three tablespoons of bleach to five litres of water. Now, when you have used bleach at this rate of dilution you must rinse everything carefully afterwards and think twice about where you are going to tip the waste – don't use the watercourse or outside drain and definitely don't tip it on to soil. (You could always look at a neighbour's garden though, especially one you don't like.) Alternatively, bottle it and take it to your council tip or flush it down the toilet. Or again dilute it further with a neutralising solution and then you can tip it into the drains. You do find that some brewers use bleach as a no-rinse sanitiser. This isn't the best way, as you have to have your levels of bleach exact and your dilution rates spot on. You also need to know the pH of the water as this can affect everything. You can use a home-brew cleaner, as these are fairly exact and do the job well, but part of the function of all my books is to show the reader how to create popular things cheaply without altering the quality – and these things do cost money. Having said that, sometimes paying out for something like a home-brew cleaning kit is a good move as you are less likely to make a complete pig's ear of the cleaning than if you start playing around with bleach.

WHAT SORT OF EQUIPMENT WILL I NEED?

Often the majority of hobbies require pieces of kit. Brewing is no different although once you have the kit you are set up for life. They are pieces that last. Some pieces are useful to have but are not necessary and I am a great believer that in these hard times it's better to improvise than go out spending a king's ransom on a tiny piece of kit. Although you will need a lot more equipment for brewing from a mash than you will for brewing from a beer kit.

THE BARE MINIMUM FOR A BREWING KIT

The basic kit you need for this is: a large kettle, long spoon, a fermenting vessel, airlock and bung, syphon tube and bottles, caps, capper and some cleaner. When you are brewing from a malt extract, add to the above a large boiling pan (a jam pan would do) and a sparge bag. If you are brewing from a mash you will need a water boiler and sparger. You can also add to your list a thermometer and a hydrometer. An insulated chest or box is useful for keeping your brew at the right temperature in the early stages. These are not essential but useful to have. The one real essential I find is to have plenty of hot water. This is the real secret of success.

KETTLE OR WATER BOILER?

This is an issue and dilemma I've come across over many, many years. I find that I favour the water boiler as it's the least likely object for my wife to throw at me when she discovers the mess I've made. Now a kettle that can boil around 5–10 litres is sufficient, but one that can boil a continuous amount is better. You will find that a boiler on continuous run will have sterilised the water by boiling it and usually holds more than the small amount found in a kettle.

Water boilers can usually handle around 25 litres of water and can be picked up fairly cheaply; it's the plumbing that is costly. When you are brewing you generally need around 19 litres of hot water from start to finish – which would involve boiling a lot of kettles. You can use a stove like an Aga, but they do tend to lose their heat quickly when the lid is off for a long time while the kettles are boiling.

Most of the equipment I'm talking about here will probably appear 'beer centric', but in fact this isn't the case because beer, mead, cider and fruit wines all need the majority of the same materials and equipment. You can buy some purpose-built devices from home-brew shops, which act as a mash turner and water boiler, and some of the hi-tech ones also can be used as a fermentation bin. These are generally made of stainless steel, with a false bottom made of fine mesh; this should be just above the draw tap as it is there to prevent the crushed grains from blocking the tap. What I like about these units is that they enable you to set and automatically maintain an accurate temperature through the mashing process.

SPARGE BAG AND SPARGER

This is also known as a grain bag, but as I said earlier the word sparge sounds rude and therefore I like to use it. 'Ooh-er Mrs, how's your sparge bag these days?' And so on . . . This bag contains the crushed grains. If you keep them in the bag it prevents contamination from entering other areas of the process. It also helps to keep them in one place whilst you mash away, and it will keep them away from the boiler element. If you don't 'sparge' you might find that your grains catch the element and burn. The taste of burnt beer isn't one that I think you will be after. Sparging itself is the process of rinsing the grains after mashing and this tends to require a lot of water – usually around 20 litres of hot water, not necessarily boiling. The hot water should be able to hit the bag and create a fine spray and vent easily. In the past I've used a variety of materials and tools – usually found in my kitchen and much to my wife's annoyance. For sparging, I used to use a well-insulated plastic bin, or a barrel with a tap on the bottom; you can get these easily from home-brew or beekeeping suppliers. This tap should be threaded so that you can fix a hose and fine shower head to it. If you go on line to a website like eBay and you can't find anything under the home-brew section, have a look at the beekeeping section as well.

INSULATED CHEST

You will need an insulated box or chest – like a camping cool box, or one of those storage boxes that you take to the shops – which will be used in the mashing process. Any insulated container will do, as long as it is capable of withstanding temperatures of around 85°C. When you are ready to use it, preheat it with hot water. It's no use putting hot beer into a cool box that's cold, as you'll be well off target for your ideal temperature, and you may find your beer doesn't process in the way you expected but may deteriorate. By heating your box first you should be able to hold your temperature at around the ideal 65°F for at least two hours.

(FERMENTING) VESSEL

If you work on the basis that you are making 40 pints (or 23 litres) of beer you are going to need a container that holds a corresponding amount. Certainly you should allow for a minimum of 25 litres, but it's better to work on the basis of about 27 to 34 litres to be on the safe side. Because of the foaming nature of the mash during fermentation you will need the expansion element in your tank. If your first brew is less than 40 pints you will still need a 27–34 litre bin. Always look for a suitable bin to use. Make sure it's easy to clean, and is made from food grade plastic. Food grade plastic is tough, durable and, if you do decide to store cheese in it one winter, by the time you come to brew in to again, all it will need is a wipe out and a swill. Non food grade plastic retains the smell of the last visitor and I don't think there's a market for Cheddar-flavoured beer. You never know though . . .

Make sure the fermentation vessel you choose is one that is easy to carry, suitable for your home environment, has a secure lid (either screw fit or clip on), and most of all has a gauge on the sides, both internal and external to show the level and quantity. I would always look for a vessel that has metric and imperial measurements on it, as if you are not of that generation that can calculate between the two you are bound to find someone who only knows one and not the other. Try to find one with a tap on the bottom, otherwise you will be siphoning the brew off through the yeast at the top and sometimes there can be cross-contamination or cloudiness – and if you are not looking for a cloudy beer (like a white or wheat beer) it can look a bit amateurish. Also look for a vessel that has a pre-bored hole in the lid to allow for the seating of a standard demijohn-size rubber bung, as you will need to fit an airlock at a later stage.

DEMIJOHNS/CARBOYS

Most glass containers that are traditional to the home brewing industry are known as demijohns and these contain a gallon of liquid, whilst the carboy contains five gallons. If I was starting brewing again and I knew then what I know now, I would always have one of each (demijohn and carboy). The reason being that you can always use a demijohn for small quantities but you would never produce small amounts in a carboy as the volume is too great, i.e. one gallon of brew and the equivalent volume of four gallons of open space, makes for a lot of gas.

I think a demijohn looks great, very traditional. They are easy to find in car boot sales and if I'm honest they have always made my garden shed or kitchen look like Dr Frankenstein's laboratory. Bubbling and belching, they tick away creating something from nothing. On the down side they are fragile, and can shatter. If you are not buying brand new then you don't know the history of them and when dealing with liquids you really don't want something full of half-fermented beer shattering and landing everywhere. Worse still, you don't want to pour a pint of beer for friends and for it to contain a shard of glass. You will also find that glass containers do not have taps on the bases either. Glass is a lot easier to clean than plastic but on the down side they usually have apertures far too small for you to get your hand in to clean, and if you are a messy puppy like me, this can be a real problem. If you are on a budget then I look for a bucket that has contained something like mayonnaise in it. You can get one free from a catering department or restaurant kitchen. You could also buy a new plastic rubbish bin and use a tightly-fitted bin bag over it as a very inexpensive way of brewing.

USING AN AIRLOCK

In essence an airlock is to allow carbon dioxide to escape during the fermentation process and at the same time it prevents air from entering the fermentation vessel. If air is allowed to gain entry you may find that it contaminates the brew. Also the gas bubbling through the airlock will give you an indication as to how the yeast is getting on, and how hard it is working. Occasionally water is drawn from the airlock into the fermentation chamber. If this is the case and the water hasn't been sterilised you may easily find that your brew is contaminated. To be on the safe side you can use pre-boiled and cooled water, but then I have also known brewers to use vodka in the fermentation lock. It doesn't have to be an expensive vodka, but certainly don't use a flavoured one. Ideally you could use any unflavoured spirit. Don't forget to use a rubber bung to seal the carboy – and make sure it's a new bung. If you buy old used kits one thing I would always do is replace any of the perishables.

USING A HYDROMETER

This is a device that measures the density of the liquid. It is composed of a long, thin, glass cylinder, which has a weight at the bottom. When the weighted end is submerged the calibrated section sticks out of the liquid at a given height, which is determined by the density of that particular liquid; gosh that sounded technical! You might have heard some of those clever home-brew drinkers or real ale aficionados discussing the specific gravity (or SG), which shows how dense the brew is. When you start the process of brewing the wort contains a lot of sugars and these little chaps develop and increase the density of the brew. This gives you the original gravity (OG). Now as the sugar is turned into alcohol its density actually decreases and the reading at the final end of the fermentation process is known as the final gravity (FG).

You really have to be aware of these gravity issues – it may all sound very technical and wordy, but it is very important. This process will give you the opportunity of calculating your alcohol content. I've spoken to a broad selection of beer, mead, wine and cider drinkers to get a rough idea of what the drinker wants. I've found, as with most things in life, the younger the person, the more extreme they choose to be. My survey found that the younger the drinker the more alcohol content they want. As the drinker matures he/she feels happier with something to be savoured, in which they can try to distinguish the subtleties and content.

When it comes to calculating the alcohol content, you really want to know how strong it is: will it make your eyes water? Or will it be so low in alcohol you might mistake it for a cup of tea? I remember going out with some friends as a young man/old teenager and trying the strongest brews. I was in Ireland and was given a lager, I think it was Skol and its ABV was really high. I didn't know this and not to be outdone by my chums, I drank it. It was really unpleasant as it felt like it was neat alcohol. A farmer in County Donegal gave me some *poitín*, with an ABV of 95% (or so he said, I didn't know what he was on about). I smiled, rude to refuse I thought, and drank away. It burned my throat and other parts of me that hadn't even come in contact with it. He smiled, drank his and then told me a batch in the 50s had made a member of his family blind. He also said that on really cold days he would use the stuff to start his tractor by placing some in the carburettor. I don't think I've been the same since . . .

To calculate the alcohol content, or ABV, first you take your OG and subtract it from your FG then multiply it by 131. Your hydrometer will help you to calculate when the brew is ready to bottle as you can use it in conjunction with the airlock. It works like this: when your airlock slows down bubbling and eventually stops, and any foam has disappeared from the surface of your brew, you are advised to take a hydrometer reading and make a record of it. Two days later take another reading and record it. If you find that the recorded amounts are the same the fermentation has finished and it's time to move on;

if the second recording is lower, then wait a further two days and repeat. If you are successful and have two identical readings then the fermentation process has finished. Your FG or final gravity reading should be below the 1010 mark. When you have successfully obtained two equal readings don't feel you have to bottle straight away – a couple more days won't harm your brew, in fact it will improve it. But a word of caution, don't leave it too long, as after three or four days it won't get any better.

You can use your hydrometer to help confirm whether the fermentation process has stalled. This can be a common problem and the hydrometer can be a useful piece of kit here. If the yeast decides to give up the ghost, the airlock will stop bubbling and the foaming will also stop. Now it's either stopped fermenting and has done so early, or it's stopped/stalled. At this stage you should wait a couple of days and take a reading (three cheers for this piece of kit I really thought I didn't need). If you get a reading of 1020 or greater, then the fermentation process has stalled and you need to return to the start to correct this.

It's dangerous out there

Don't get all anal about your hydrometer readings because every time you open the lid to take a reading you let airborne nasties in that can contaminate your brew. I always check the gravity when I've added my yeast, and then I leave it until the bubbling stops and don't interfere. It is so easy to want to keep returning and have a look and a poke but you're not doing your brew any favours. I've been asked a number of times about why brews have stalled or died and it's generally because it's been interfered with. Leave it alone and nature will sort it out. Most damaged brews are because of over interference. If you are using the same hydrometer between several brews, always clean it before you test again.

When you remove a sample of wort for testing don't use the hydrometer in the fermentation vessel, take your sample by using a sterile syphon to draw off the wort into a hydrometer jar and float the hydrometer in this. A word of advice, as I've fallen foul of this in the past: when you are putting the meter in the hydrometer jar, lower it in slowly. I say this because often excited brewers will drop the meter and, depending on the consistency of the brew, it will shatter. Let it drop slowly. Now when it is in the jar, gently spin the meter to remove any unwanted air bubbles. Once the meter has stopped spinning, take your reading. Once you have taken your reading discard the wort, don't ever return it. Always have a thermometer to hand; it's a useful tool but not half as useful as a hydrometer. I've taken my hydrometer to the theatre, on holiday to Vietnam, and even set up an account for it with the TSB; it even has pocket money. God that beer was strong stuff.

BOTTLING YOUR BREW

Filling equipment

When you bottle your prized brew it must be done quickly and smoothly, to prevent any spillage and to stop any other foreign bodies from entering the mix. Use a length of rubber tubing to syphon off the mix, as with this you can control the flow and the amount of foam that's going into your filling vessels. If you choose to pour it out you will regret it as there will be a mass of foam and your kitchen will smell like an old pub. A rubber tube will also reduce the amount of contamination or infection. You can buy a little bit of kit that goes on to the bottom of the fermentation bin and has a small length of rubber tubing on it. You can then push the bottle all the way up to its neck, open the valve and then control the flow and the amount of head that is going into the bottle. If you don't have the magical tap on the bottom of your bin I would invest in a sturdy handled jug and decant the brew into each bottle. Don't go for a plastic jug because the surface will crease and graze. Use a glass or metal jug and, if you have the choice, I would plump for metal. I would always opt for a sediment trap on the fermentation bin (this is a long and j-shaped tube), as this will also help to reduce the sediment collection.

Vessels to store it in

There are a variety of vessels that you can store your treasured brew in – whether you are making wine, beer, mead or cider, you will always need something to store it in. Unless you are planning to rule the world of home brewing, a keg may be a step too far; they are also very expensive.

As I write this book I am frantically bottling a very nice, very cloudy and slightly too gassy wheat beer. A recipe was sent from my German brother-in-law with the strict instructions only to use X, Y and Z. He also warned me that it might make me burp a lot, so let's wait and see. I'm also deeply involved with making some wines out of pea pods and the flavours and content over the last few years have been superb. Obviously there's the obligatory mead. Being a beekeeper, making mead has become second nature, and my wife is finishing off some elderflower cordial. I can see myself on those late autumn and winter nights, cuddled around the fire, with a nice pint of heady wheat beer in one hand and a chip butty in the other, and God staring down on me.

If you have brewed sufficient to fill a standard five-gallon bin of home brew then you will be looking for 45 × 500 ml bottles to decant it into. I always stay with one type and size of bottle, as this makes it really easy to store. I wouldn't be bothered collecting old beer bottles as they are designed to be used once and then ditched. Wine bottles are OK to reuse but commercial beers tend to have their gases controlled and therefore the bottles have thinner, cheaper glass. If you've got a fiery, volatile brew, the glass may not be suitable. You can use those beer bottles that have been conditioned or even those that have a covered sprung cap.

Always use brown bottles. There is a good reason for this: it's because tinted glass, especially brown (I always thought brown was a dull choice, such a disappointing colour) protects the contents of beer. The frequency of light is disrupted by the brown glass; green glass is used for wine, for similar reasons. But for beer the glass protects the contents against photochemistry, which has a tendency to alter the beer's quality. Both sunlight and artificial light may interact with the hop compounds and will produce almost a foul smell, which won't enhance your brew. Green glass offers better protection than clear, but not as good as brown.

This deterioration of flavour and smell in your beer can take place within a few minutes of light exposure, especially in strong sunlight, so if you are living anywhere north of Coventry you have nothing to worry about. But having said this, you could decant your brew into clear or green bottles as long as you keep them in a dark cupboard, or under the stairs perhaps. One thing I like about using clear glass is that at least you can observe the yeast and what it is doing, the fermentation, and how much gas is in there. You tend not to be able to do that when you are dealing with green and especially brown glass.

When it comes to bottles, saving them is cheaper than buying them, but it does mean you will have an eclectic mix of shapes and sizes. You can use a number of the higher quality end of the disposable fizzy pop bottles, the ones that Coca Cola/Pepsi or lemonade comes in. You will find that these bottles are easy to obtain and are very popular with brewers. You can also find many that are brown, for example those that have had dandelion and burdock in. Unless you can get coloured plastic, the clear ones will be the most common and will need to be stored in the usual dark corner. These plastic bottles are cheap, easy to find, you don't need a capper as the screw caps are quickly sealed, they are easy to wash and maintain and don't shatter when you drop them. All isn't roses though, as there are issues with plastic bottles. These sorts of bottles are a little porous to oxygen and in turn will lose flavour. Also, it's difficult to convince yourself that you are drinking draught beer out of a pop bottle. Beer in a pop bottle will be OK for up to three months but after that it's going to start to deteriorate. Glass is your only option if you are looking to lay some beer down for your granddaughter's wedding. I mentioned a bottle capper earlier, you don't need one of these obviously with a screw cap but if you are doing glass bottles you will need one. Bottle cappers are machines that hammer or force the cap on to the top of the bottle and form a seal.

Let's have a look at some beer recipes now. These are all basic and straightforward – and should be a breeze to produce if you've read the preceding chapter carefully! As these are very old, tried and tested recipes, they are given in imperial measurements – you can convert them to metric if you want to, but they've worked well for me like this so I see no need to change them.

WINTER SPECIAL BREW

Ingredients

6 lbs dark malt extract
3 lbs dry dark malt extract

2 lbs wildflower honey
½ lb chocolate malt
½ lb black malt
½ lb Munich malt
½ lb flaked barley
½ lb malto dextrin
7 cloves
3 oranges
3 sticks of cinnamon
2 whole nutmegs
2 oz grated ginger
⅓ cup molasses
2 oz cascade hops (whole leaf)
1 oz Galena hops

Method

Mash all the grains for 30 min. Add the malt extract, honey, molasses and the galena hops and boil for 30 minutes. Add 1 oz of the cascade hops along with all the herbs and oranges to the boil for another 25 minutes, adding the remaining 1 oz cascade hops during the last 10 minutes of the boil, for aromatics. Cool the wort down and strain out the oranges and hops and everything before dumping into the primary fermenter.

DARK BEER

Ingredients

3⅓ lbs Munton and Fison old ale kit malt extract
2½ lbs Munton and Fison light dry malt extract

6 oz black patent malt
6 oz roasted barley
6 oz caramel malt 40 degree
1 ½ oz Nugget hops – 60 minutes
½ oz Nugget hops – 10 minutes
1 ½ teaspoons gypsum
1 packet Red Star champagne yeast
2 oz corn sugar to prime
Boiling time 60 minutes
Primary fermentation 7 weeks at 70 degrees
Secondary fermentation 6 weeks at 70 degrees

Method

Crush grains and add to 3 quarts cold water. Slowly raise temperature to gentle simmer and hold for 10 minutes. Sparge with 2 quarts hot water. Add to brewpot to make 3 gallons. Heat to boil and add malt extract.

BASIC PILSNER

This is a really straightforward and easy recipe, and has a superb flavour and taste.

Ingredients

6⅔ lbs light malt extract
2½ ounces Spalt hops for bittering
1 oz Saaz hops for aroma
1 teaspoon Irish moss
1 package Munich lager yeast
¾ cup corn sugar for priming

Method

Bring water to boil and add malt extract and Spalt hops. Boil for 1 hour adding the Saaz hops and Irish Moss for the last 10 minutes. Cool the wort and pitch the yeast.

Primary ferment at 50 to 55 degrees for 5 to 7 days. Transfer to secondary fermenter. Lager for 3 to 4 weeks (*Lager* is actually German for cellar). Bottle using corn sugar. Age your beer in the bottle for 7 to 10 days before you drink it.

BASIC BITTER

This is a really easy bitter recipe that should give you a bitter at high street quality and not high street prices.

Ingredients

3 lbs light malt extract – this is usually 1 can
2 lbs light dry malt
1 ½ oz Kent Goldings hops for boiling
1 oz Cascade hops for finish
2 teaspoons gypsum
1 teaspoon Irish Moss
1 package London ale yeast
½ cup corn sugar for priming

Method

Combine malt extracts, gypsum and Kent Goldings hops in water and boil for 1 hour. Add 1oz Cascade hops and Irish Moss for the last 5 minutes of the boil. Cool the wort and pitch the yeast.

Fermentation should be complete within 10 days. Bottle using corn sugar. Age in the bottle for 5 to 7 days.

CHAPTER 11

IRELAND ON MY MIND, AND MY LIVER

Once I had left home I went to visit my uncle in Ireland (I'm protecting his name for legal reasons but I don't think you can indict the dead). He took me into his barn (byre) and showed me his illegal still. It was a collection of copper pipes, a bath, glassware and one of his prize cows close by. I had been shown this because when I had asked him about poitín (potato whiskey), from an early age he always told me that the 'little people' delivered it. All I had to do was ask them and they would leave me some. In fact it was Liam the milkman. You left a note saying how many bottles of milk you wanted and, if you asked for 'an extra', along came some of the wonder stuff.

By the time I was in my early twenties and travelling I finally asked my uncle about potato whiskey. He drew some off and gave it to me to try; I can only say it tasted like what it was. Neat and clear with alcohol at around 100% proof, it stripped the enamel from my teeth and burnt my throat leaving me bereft of any ability to taste and swallow for around three days. My uncle smiled and slapped me on the back and laughed. This was Uncle Sean's breakfast. When I saw him starting the old tractor on it on a cold frosty morning I knew I had narrowly escaped death.

One sunny day, it must have been a Wednesday because every other day it rains, up popped a man and a woman, more of a young girl really. Both wore the uniforms of the *Gardai* (police). The older chap was clearly in charge, he greeted my uncle in Gaelic and then continued his conversation in English. He told him that a fax had been received from *Gardai Siochana* in Dublin (the Irish equivalent to Scotland Yard), to look for illegal stills. I flinched yet my uncle stayed still and motionless. The guard walked towards the byre and told my uncle that he would be back on Thursday to inspect his outbuildings. The *bhngard* (policewoman) turned in disbelief at her superior and we heard her say that they should inspect now. When they had gone we moved the still over the lane to Mr Dumfy's byre and secreted it behind some bales of hay. Inside the byre there were four other stills that my uncle identified as belonging to friends and neighbours of his. On their return the guard consulted his clipboard and ticked several boxes to say that he hadn't found a still or any equipment for the making of illegal whiskey. The *bhngard* just shook her head. My uncle asked where the guard was going next. 'To Mr Dumfy's,' was the reply. I panicked as I knew there were several stills in there and enough contraband to put many of the people of the county in prison for several years, but my uncle said nothing. 'I'm going to tell him I will be around a week on Tuesday,' and off he went. A search of an area the size of Yorkshire did not produce a single still. Months later my uncle and cousins were in the local pub, skulling pints, when the guard came in, off duty of course. A pint was produced for him and two bottles of *poitín*. It wasn't seen as breaking the law, just enforcing a country way of policing. Steer clear of the *poitín*, it's strong stuff and bad stuff can blind you.

CHAPTER 12

MAKING COUNTRY WINES

I spent a lot of time growing up in Ireland and in Ireland's second city, Liverpool. As a country boy in the city I found it really difficult at times to fit in. But the constant throughout my childhood and youth was the love of the countryside and everything it had to offer. I would find myself slipping off to country parks, coastal retreats and getting lost in the woods and dunes.

On my returns to Ireland I would be confronted by a rural society beautifully lost in the twentieth century and not appearing to want to catch up with her neighbour. I remember one visit to Ireland to be greeted by Mrs Murphy. Mrs Murphy lived in a static caravan that she liked to call a Swiss chalet. She grew all sorts of fruit and vegetables and would dish them out to those she considered to be the needy in the community; in reality she was poor herself. At Pol du in Garten where she lived I found her tending her patch. When I called her she turned around sporting one of the largest courgettes I've ever seen. She told me that she was going to make courgette wine from it – now to me I would rather sleep in a nettle field. Most of what she grew she told me went to the poor and what was left behind went into her liver. She made wines and potions out of everything she could find. She lived until she was 98 and never had a day's illness or complaint. Pat Murphy would have been burnt at the stake a few hundred years earlier, but when the local doctor isn't really that local, you have a tendency to pray a lot and visit the local wise woman.

Any country wine can be made with most fruits with an ample flesh. You can make a tea wine but that's another story. Have a wander around your local fruit shop to see what is out and when, and what is going cheaply. I have a tendency to buy Sharon fruit when they come down in price and are nice and ripe and full of their own natural fruit sugars. Often I find myself out with my friend Trevor sourcing our fruits in the hedgerow – blackberries, elderberries or whortleberries. I've known Trevor find dandelions in spring, oak leaves in autumn and rhubarb in early summer. The one thing Pat Murphy told me was that as long as you brewed it long enough it should be safe. But master the basics first: if you don't, because you are using some thick woody fruits and vegetables you will find that your wine can be rough and a little unpleasant. After that the sky's the limit.

You must give your young wines at least six to twelve months to come to strength. It's the acids found in grape-based wines that give them a good flavour and strength. Some fruits and vegetables that I'm going to talk about are really quite low in acid so you will need time to assist you. At times you might need to add wine acid to correct the problem and give it a lift.

FIRST THINGS THIRST

If you decide to make a country wine you really don't want to lose the flavour of what it is you are producing. I once watched Richard Briers as Tom Good in the *Good Life* when he made a pea pod Burgundy. The audience laughed. If you are adventurous, this is one I certainly would try as it has such a great taste. As I said earlier, because of the low acid content of some of the ingredients you might need to add some wine acid but not too much as you will lose that beautiful pea pod or delicate elderflower flavour. Mrs Murphy taught me well and I've found that the majority of the wines I've produced over the years have ranged over strength, colour and volume. But they've remained true to the fact they are non-grape wines and true to the fact they are drinkable as a wine. There's no stigma associated with a wine made from elderflower that has the same volume, clarity and superior flavour of a Pinot Grigio just because it doesn't come in a stuck up label. I would hope that any budding or professional wine producer would care to look around their land and not just focus on the grape or readily identifiable crop but look further afield and consider what could be a welcome addition to his brew. You should be able to look at the herbs, flowers and even weeds to examine what could make a beautiful fruity wine or a joyous addition. You might find yourself ridiculed for brewing away from the norm, but in reality those wine makers who are more than happy to experiment and combine interesting flavours and alcohol levels are the ones who have most fun.

MY FISH WAS T H I S BIG

Remember year on year you can produce the same wine from the same produce and with the same water and it will be different every time. You will often be in the company of others who will taste a wine, look at a jar of honey or talk about a holiday and will always say that it wasn't the same as last year or the year before. They are right, it wasn't the same; it may have been neither better nor worse, but it wasn't the same. That's because of the weather, which affects the sugar contents of the fruit or vegetable, the formation of the fruit, the amount of nutrients that have been released from the soil through an unusual heavy downpour or the slow release through a particularly dry spell. But the one thing that all these products have in common is that the previous year's was always better than this year's.

APPLE WINE

One of the favourite country wines I have ever had to comment on has been the apple wine. As I write this book in rural Lancashire, I can see the apple tree in the garden bent over with fruit. Large green and red skinned apples, juicy to look at and even juicier to eat, roll gently on the bough as the early autumn wind makes them rock on their stalks. At this time of year all the apples come out all in one flush and so many are left behind, discarded or turned to compost.

It was with a friend that we discovered the joy of not just making apple wine but also drinking it. It's a delightful full flavoured, crisp wine that would be smooth on the palate and gentle on the throat. This shouldn't be, or be treated as a thin cider or scrumpy; this is a totally different kettle of fish and should be treated as a wine and produced accordingly. You must sterilise all your equipment otherwise this will have an effect on how your wine turns out. You don't have to select the best apples or those with a guaranteed flavour; you should always work with baking or part bakers in your wine making as they will have a lower sugar content and usually a greater acid content. You could use dessert apples but they will alter the flavour and you will need to alter the amount of apples, so in this instance stick with the bakers.

Ingredients

1 kg sugar, preferably granulated
4.5 litres of cold water (tap water is OK unless you live in a very hard water area like the south east of England or parts of the Home Counties. If you are unsure as to whether you have hard water then a general rule of thumb is if you have any of the following: Do you need a filter on your kettle? Does your soap fail to lather in the bath? Do you have white fur on your water pipes?)
1.5 kg cooking apples
2 unwaxed lemons
1 orange
1 teaspoon wine yeast
Pinch of yeast nutrient
Some pectin enzyme.

Method

Wash your apples, and cut them but don't bother peeling or coring them. I always mince the apples as you get a consistent flavour. If you just chop, some pieces will be slower to cook than others. Put the minced mess in to a sterilised plastic bucket and then pour the cold water over it. Cover your bucket and leave it for at least a week. Leave it in a dark undisturbed place. I always like under the stairs but then I've used it so many times my wife knows where to find me so I have to find somewhere else to hide. As for a cover over the bucket, don't use a tea towel, as I find they tend to attract dust, and they have a habit of slipping and falling into the mix. I always like to use either some tin foil or even better a shower cap. If you know someone who travels a lot and stays in hotels ask them to collect shower caps for you. When I used to stay in a lot of hotels my wife, the present Mrs Hughes, would ask me for shower caps; I found she was using them for proving bread over the Aga.

Give your bucket a good daily stir with a clean plastic spoon – a large jam spoon would work well. After a week, strain your goop through a muslin bag straight into another sterilised plastic bucket. Then add your sugar and the juice and grated rinds of the citrus fruits. Add the yeast, the pectin and the yeast nutrient, about a good pinch for this amount of yeast. Cover your bucket again with whatever top you choose and leave for at least 24 hours, but not too long though. Strain your liquid, and press all the liquid you can out of the mush using the back of your fat spoon, or use your hand (in a clean disposable plastic glove). Drain the liquid into a fermentation vessel. You can drink it straight away as a yummy non-alcoholic drink, let's say a mature apple juice, or leave it for at least four months in a cool dark place until it turns into a clear yumptious wine.

BEETROOT WINE

Recently I spent time in France, in the company of my friends Hélène and Franck Terminière, and they were kind enough to let me taste some of their brews. One of the greatest of experiences was when they showed me what they brewed to keep them warm in the long winter months. After several hours of steadily becoming sloshed, we fell asleep in a big heap, dogs, cats and empty bottles.

In the morning, no hangover, no dryness of the mouth, no aversion to a fry up. So I asked the Terminières if I could have the recipes for the drinks from the night before, as I was halfway through writing a book on drinks; and out she pulled pieces of paper, cardboard and a series of books and hurriedly wrote down what I needed.

We had started off with a delicious red wine that looked the colour of Vimto. For those of you living outside of England Vimto is . . . Vimto. There's no comparison. It's a medium coloured soft drink and

Hélène had brewed something with the same colour, taste, sweetness and delicacy; but with alcohol. What she had given us was *vin betterave*, which turned out to be beetroot wine, yumpster. This wine looked just the colour of beetroot. That wet, shiny, deep red, if not burgundy-coloured vegetable had now been transformed into one of the nicest wines I had ever tasted. Hélène talked me through the process. She said that it was always better to use beetroot at the start of the season when they are sweet or mid-season when they are just ready to roast. If they are too old they will make the wine taste like wood. Beetroot has a low sugar content, so for the yeast to convert the sugar into alcohol it is important to keep any additional oxygen out of the fermentation vessel. You achieve this by keeping the vessel completely airtight. Ensure that these bottles are not entirely filled to the brim but have a little room for expansion. Once you've made your wine it can be drunk straight away, but the longer you leave it, the darker and stronger it will become. It should go from a Beaujolais to a Rioja over a period of years, and will be vinegar by the time it's about ten. As a sweet but not a dessert wine it's all down to taste; you can lift the sweetness level of the wine by the addition of further sugars. I have a habit of making this wine in mid spring with long dark winter evenings in mind. Made in spring and allowed to ferment, by the time the clocks go back you can find yourself with a nice port to sip on next to an open fire with a chip butty in your hand. (If you are American and don't understand what a chip butty is, well it's the food of the Gods.)

Ingredients

1 kg beetroot
1 kg granulated sugar
2 small unwaxed lemons
3.5 litres water

4 sticks of cinnamon
6 cloves
Half a cup of warm water and a teaspoon of yeast

Method

I always find preparing wine is best done á la Ken Dodd. That is, every time you complete a function come out with a catchphrase like, 'By Jove, Mrs!' or, 'How tickled I am!'. This will ensure no one enters the kitchen or steals your wine. Now you will need to wash your beets. 'By Jove, Mrs!' Well, you get the gist. Peel off the skins and finely grate the beets. Dissolve your yeast in half a cup of warm water and mix in half a teaspoon of sugar and leave to rise. You will then need to boil the 3.5 litres of water in a clean pan and add the grated beetroot and leave it to cook. Keep the pan at a rolling boil until the beetroot is soft. Take it off the boil and leave to one side until it is around a lukewarm temperature. Strain through a clean boiled muslin bag directly into a sterilised container, then add your sugar to the drained liquid and stir until all the sugar has dissolved. Next add your citrus juices, the dissolved yeast, water and spices. As a must the container must be airtight and stored once again where the wife doesn't look (somewhere dark, clean and away from disturbance to allow it the luxury of fermentation to take place), generally for around 15 days. Around the fourth or fifth day, open the container and give it a gentle stir with a wooden spoon (plastic is fine, but try to avoid using a metal one). From then on leave it alone to carry on fermenting. Don't disturb it again and leave it be until the 15th day. Once the fermentation process is over, strain the mix well. Try to allow the liquor to flow but try not to break up any residue, as it will cause the wine to become cloudy. Once strained, pour into sterilised bottles. You may wish to store your wine somewhere cool and dark but it's just as good if it's stored in a pantry or shed. Enjoy!

SAP WINES

As the evening with Hélène and Franck wore on I could have sworn that the next brew was poured from a copper pipe. But then I guess that was the drink confusing me. I asked what I was drinking and the best translation I could get was tree sap. Now when I returned to Blighty I looked up the translation again, only to find that it was indeed birch sap. I can't be too sure, but I think it was common birch, because silver birch has always been considered to be poisonous.

Hélène told me that this wine could be made from a variety of saps and is centuries old. After a little research back in Lancashire I discovered that this wine was had been very common for hundreds of years but appeared to have died out. In France it was a little underground but still active. Saps from a variety of trees can be used to make a selection of goods, from beer to vinegar. I asked her when was the best time to collect sap, thinking of the old adage about sap rising in the spring, young man's pleasures etc. In the spring, she told me. You collect the sap as the days start to warm up, the sap rises and you trap it before the leaves open. She whisked me off to one of the birches in her fields and showed me exactly what to do. You drill a hole into the bark of the tree to a depth of no more than 6 mm. You shouldn't break into the flesh of the tree, only into the bark. Force a clear plastic tube into the hole and secure it. Place the other end of the tube into a glass bottle with a hole drilled into the cap. Or you can go for the larger version where you don't need to keep revisiting the bottle: use the same gauge piping but run it into a 5 litre container, and using a 5cm auger drill bore a hole into the corresponding cork; fit the cork and pipe together and bung up the container and let nature do its work. You can easily get five litres from a tree, sometimes more depending on the spring climate. This is the same approach as for obtaining rubber sap. You basically bleed the tree. It doesn't do the tree any harm unless you use multiples and force the tree to produce too much. In this case you will make the tree weak, the sap will be substandard, and it's likely that the tree will go into shock, therefore not producing enough sap to open the leaves and will die. Don't be greedy with this wine/beer; work with nature. A word of advice, leave a little hole for the air to escape, otherwise you might find your container growing at an alarming rate of knots.

It's not over yet . . . Don a fez and make Tommy Cooper noises to assist in the flow of the sap. Leave the container on a supported base and if the conditions are suitable, within a minimum of two days, hey presto, a gallon or five litres of sap. When you have enough, remove the piping from the bark and remember to plug the hole with a small cork. You will need to do this as the bark of a tree is essentially its skin. Apart from allowing infection in to the tree, you will find that as the sap flows out of the hole a variety of insects will collect around it and create further damage. If you use a cork and not a plastic one this will be better for the tree as she will quickly absorb the cork into the bark and continue to grow and develop. This is why I always say that we should work with nature and not against it. All the answers in life can be found in nature.

What you have to remember about tree sap is that its sugar level is rather low. So you will have to adjust the sweetness required. You generally find that for every five litres there is approximately 100 g of sugar.

Ingredients

You need around 4.5 litres of sap
250 g finely chopped raisins
1 kg granulated white sugar

Juice of 2 lemons
1 sachet of all-purpose yeast

Method

Boil the sap in a decent sized thick-bottomed pan; a jam pan is fine. You should start using the sap fairly quickly after you have harvested it as it has a tendency to go off quickly. Add your sugar to the boiling sap and allow to simmer for ten minutes. Be careful with this mix as boiling sugar and a substance with sugar in it has a tendency to spit. If you get boiling sugar on your skin it will really hurt and leave a nasty scar. I speak from personal experience. Add the chopped raisins to a sterilised plastic bucket. You can use a sterilising tablet rather than very hot water as the water has a tendency to draw out some of the taste of the plastic which then infuses the liquor. Again there are always alternatives open to you here. If you want to use a plastic bucket but don't fancy using a sterilisation tablet, put boiling water in to the plastic bucket several times, rinse it out and keep replacing until the water can be drunk without any plastic taste or taint.

So, pour the boiling sugary liquid on to the raisins and then add your lemon juice. Empty the contents of your packet of yeast into a clean clear glass and start it off with some water. Allow the sugary mix (not the yeast) to cool to blood temperature and then add the yeast to the mix. Now I find it best to leave it in a covered bucket, preferably with a corresponding plastic lid, for around three days. Then strain it off into a 4.5 litre jar or fermentation vessel and seal it off with an airlock. Again, leave it somewhere dark, this time preferably somewhere warm like an airing cupboard, until the fermentation process has finished.

At this stage you need to rack the wine off into a clean jar and leave it, preferably on a raised platform so as to be able to see the completion of the settlement. It's of no use to you if you are waiting for the settlement to drop to the bottom of the jar if every other day you are tilting it to see if it's settled and you keep on mixing it up again. Another way of checking the clarity of your wine is to use a small torch. Place the torch lens against the back of the jar and turn it on. You will be able to see straight away whether there is anything floating, or rising, in your wine without lifting it a single millimetre. If you are concerned about filtering and sediment, use a clean, freshly-boiled muslin bag to filter it through. And finally, bottle in clean, sterilised bottles, use clean new corks and store in a cool dark place.

You can successfully drink this king of wines within a month, but personally I would always wait around six months. I have found on occasions that the sap has been a little on the dry side so I've had to add a little more sugar syrup. This doesn't have to be sap syrup, you can boil up a sugar syrup from two parts sugar to one part water.

RED CLOVER WINE

This was another favourite wine that Franck Terminière especially enjoyed. He explained that you could use other clovers, either fresh or dried. You need to collect your flowers early in the morning. There is a reason for this. You want the dew to have evaporated but the nectar to remain. Also if you are going to make this wine, never pick your clover or flowers on a corner or near a post or tree. Dogs have a tendency to pee on uprights and the thought of additional flavours passes me by. After picking the flowers remove the stalks and wash the flower heads thoroughly. Franck further explained that you can make this at any time of the year so long as you dry your flowers out properly. Here's how to do it: start by laying the flowers on a clean baking tray and place them in the bottom of the oven on the lowest setting; plate warming setting is good. Turn your flowers every 2–3 hours until they are completely dry. Then place them in a clear plastic bag and use when needed.

Ingredients

2 litres of red clover heads
Half a litre of white grape juice (if you are using concentrate then dilute to the half litre)
1 kg white granulated sugar
2 teaspoons acid blend
1 teaspoon yeast nutrient
A quarter of a teaspoon tannin
4.5litres water
A pinch of wine yeast
If you are unsure where you may be able to obtain some of the more exotic ingredients like wine yeast etc., there is nearly always A home-brew shop in every town, or you can buy most things online these days.

Method

Now remove all the stems of the flowers, just leaving the heads, and give them a really good wash to dislodge any unwanted guests. Dandelions are renowned for harbouring earwigs. How do you translate earwig? However, straight away they knew what I was on about, making pincing movements with their thumb and index finger. (By the way, it's '*perce-oreille*' in French, the one who pierces the ear.) Next place all your flowers in your primary fermenting vessel and pour the boiling water over them. Always ensure your vessels are clean before starting a job like this. Then add your grape juice, your acid blend, yeast nutrient, tannin and water to level out at 4.5 litres in total. When the mix is warm add your yeast, cover it with a plastic lid, tin foil or a shower cap (see above in the method for apple wine), and leave it to ferment. Don't bother it, knock it or stir it.

After a week, strain the liquid through a muslin bag and pour into a second demijohn – don't forget to fit the airlock. After two months, your next job is to syphon off, top up with a little water, refit the airlock and leave for four months. Now once your bubbles have ceased to appear in the airlock your wine should be clear. Wait for up to two weeks, sweeten if it's too dry and bottle. This is a superb wine that will surprise your friends when you tell them what it's made from.

CHERRY WINE

This has always been a firm favourite of mine. If you've had a great summer like we've had this year, then when you have an abundance of cherries there are only so many cherry pies and Elvis impressions a boy can suffer. Try making some beautiful cherry wine.

Ingredients

1 gallon or 4.5 litres water
1.5 kg sugar
1.5 kg fresh cherries
2 lemons (unwaxed)
2 teaspoons yeast

Method

You should only pick the cherries when they are fully ripe. You can tell when this is by pressing your thumb or finger into them. The flesh should return – if it doesn't return then it is bruising and the sugars are disintegrating and not distributing fully. Picking fresh is always better than getting them from the shop, as you tend to get a lot of bruised ones. Cherries are quite common and many people see them and disbelieve they are what they are. A good sign that you have struck gold is an unusually high amount of wasps on the fermenting ones that have fallen. Remember those imported shop-bought ones will be much sweeter as they will have more than likely come from Turkey or Spain. With imported cherries you will need to adjust your sugar amounts for your wine, otherwise you will produce a wine far too sweet.

When you do find the ones you want, pick and remove the stalks. Place in a clean bucket. (I know I say this time after time but you would be surprised the amount of people who contact me and tell me their wine isn't as they imagined it to be. And when you work backwards they've used a mucky old bucket that's had engine oil in it or worse.) Using a clean bucket, pour three quarters or 75% of your boiled water over the fruit. When it cools sufficiently so that you can put your finger in without it hurting, you will need to mash it with your hands. This is not an unpleasant experience, but please make sure your hands and nails are clean. Next cover the mix and leave it to stand for three days. After that, squeeze the mix through a wine bag, available at all good wine bag shops or home-brew stores. Taking the remaining quarter of the water, add the sugar and make a mix of a stock or sugar syrup. Add this to your fruit mash, and make sure it is clearly mixed together. Put it in a clean demijohn.

Next grate your lemon. Try to avoid any of the flesh getting into mix, all you want is the zest. Squeeze the rest of the lemon through a sieve and add this also. You should now have the majority of your ingredients in the mix and it should be a rather pleasant colour. Make up your yeast starter and add this also. Give it a damn good stir and seal the demijohn off with a cotton wool bung and ignore it for a further three days. Remove the cotton wool and replace it with an airlock, and again leave it alone, this time for around 12 weeks. When the fermentation process has come to an end, and you can tell this because there won't be any bubbles rising in the airlock, syphon off into clean bottles and store in a warm dark place for around 12 to 16 weeks before getting smashed.

GORSE FLOWER WINE

Now there's a saying in the United Kingdom, that when gorse isn't flowering, kissing is out of fashion. Gorse makes a nice clear gentle honey so I wasn't surprised to find out that it made a champion wine. Gorse grows almost everywhere. You can find it in people's gardens, and from wasteland and motorway embankments to the moors. It is a very versatile plant that enjoys well-drained soil and yet up on the moors it copes really well with the harsher soils and climate. Gorse is supposed to flower March to June, but as I write this book in mid October I could show you some common land not too far away where there are several gorse bushes just finishing off flowering. I've seen it out on motorway embankments near Blackpool in January. Maybe it's global warming, I don't know, but it's a shame not to take advantage of its flowers.

I was told recently that a long time ago these flowers were used to flavour whisky. I'm quite keen to try that. But as with everything that gives it also takes. Gorse bushes have nasty large thorns that seem to be able to find the gap between nail and finger every time. Always wear thick gardening gloves and always pick the fullest open flowers to get the best from this bush.

Ingredients

2 litres fully-opened gorse flowers
1 kg white granulated sugar
4.5 litres water
2 lemons, unwaxed
2 oranges
Some wine yeast

Method

Right children, start your yeast off as per the norm. Whilst you are waiting for the yeast to react, simmer your washed flowers for 15 minutes and then dissolve the sugar into the water. Next pour your mix into a clean plastic bucket and add the juices of the citrus fruits, including very thinly peeled zest. You now want to allow the mix to cool and settle to around blood temperature. Then add your yeast and leave to stand for at least three days with a cover over it. After three days strain off the solids and pour the liquid into a fermentation vessel. Fit your ever-faithful airlock and leave to ferment. When fermentation has completed, you should rack it off into a clean jar and make the amount up to its full level by using cold boiled water. Leave it for around four weeks and then filter it off and bottle in clean sterilised bottles.

COLTSFOOT WINE

I have never tried this type of wine but have eaten lots of coltsfoot rock as a child. So I was surprised when a neighbour thrust a recipe into my hand whilst I was having a quick pint in my local pub, the White Bull. Coltsfoot is a herb found throughout the UK. It likes waste ground, rough land and grows in the same sort of environment as nettles. It produces a beautiful flower around March and April. When the flower disappears and the leaves sprout, pick them and dry them in the usual manner.

Ingredients

3 litres coltsfoot flowers and/or leaves
1 kg granulated white sugar
4.5 litres water
2 lemons, juiced
Some wine yeast

Method

Once you have dried the flowers and/or leaves, place them in a clean plastic bucket and pour two litres of boiling water over them and allow them to soak for at least 24 hours. As the leaves and flowers reconstitute you will find that they float to the top, so to get the maximum amount of flavour from them keep pushing them under with a plastic or wooden spoon. Follow the method as for red clover wine from this point.

DANDELION WINE

Many people believe that a dandelion is a weed and an unwanted visitor. In fact the dandelion is a perennial herb that has the fourth highest amount of nectar for bees and is a nice addition to the table. If you don't know the story about the dandelion name it is French in origin and comes from *dent de lion*, the tooth of the lion. The French say that the petals of the flower look like sharp teeth. And the word for teeth in French is *dent*, which is related to our word dentist. So there you are. You can find dandelion flowers from around early April in abundance, but you can usually find dandelions most of the year. You will struggle to find them in the cold months but dandelion wine is a fairly delicate one and I would consider it to be a warm summer month's wine, not a robust winter warmer. When you pick the flowers, pick them on a sunny day because the flowers respond to sunshine and warmth. They are at their optimum when it is a warm day and the flowers are fully open. Pick them just were the head ends and the stalk begins. The reason for this is that the stalks contain a sticky contaminant, which is like bitter milk, and if you get it into the wine it will ruin the flavour. As for the flavour it's not one that I personally particularly like. It has a rather resinous flavour, but a bit like a number of meads such as hydromel, if the first taste doesn't always gel, the second time it gets better and grows on you.

Ingredients

(for a dry wine)
(Remember to dry your heads first. Then you can ensure the sap is dry and removed and you will be able to crush the flowers by rubbing them between two dry tea towels and allowing the petals to fall to a container or tray.)
3 quarts of dandelion petals
675 g granulated white sugar
285 ml freshly brewed strong tea like Yorkshire Tea or Typhoo
5 ml citric acid
A few drops of pectolase
Water (as in the method)
2 oranges
Wine yeast and nutrient
450 g sultanas

(for a medium wine)
Note the changes please:
1 kg white granulated sugar

(for a sweet wine)
4 quarts of dandelion petals
1.1 kg white granulated sugar

Method

For all three wines:
Place your flowers in a fermenting vessel along with the finely chopped sultanas, tea, sugar and citric acid. Add four litres of boiling water. Then with a plastic or wooden spoon stir the mix to ensure the sugar has dissolved. Cover the vessel and leave to cool until around a lukewarm temperature. Next, stir in the yeast nutrient and the pectolase, grate your orange rind (better to use unwaxed oranges for this) and press the juice out with your hand and add it to the mix. Add a lid and leave it in a warm place to ferment. Sometimes even a cool area that has a fridge/freezer in it will work so long as you leave the vessel near to the motor. Leave it alone to ferment for around nine days. Stir it at least once a day. Now you will need to strain it through a fine muslin bag and press out any solids. Clear your fermenting vessel with a quick swill and return the mix to the vessel. You will now need to cover it a second time, returning it to your warm place, and leave it to continue fermenting for around a week. After a week pour it gently into a five litre jar. If you do have a steady hand you should be able to decant the liqueur without pouring the sediment in as well. Fill up to the neck and if you are a little short of liquor use some boiled, cooled water to top it up with. Next fit a fermentation lock and leave until the fermentation process has ceased – i.e. once the rapid bubbling in the airlock on the head of the

fermentation vessel has calmed down. Then remove the airlock and decant into sterilised bottles. This wine is one that certainly improves with age. Just like my wife, or so she tells me.

ELDERFLOWER WINE (SPARKLING)

As spring turns from the unpredictable weather to the more obvious, you can start to look at what the hedgerow can offer. One of my real favourites has to be the elderflower. For such a long time the elderflower has been a major part of the rural calendar. It has influenced a variety of things from beer and cheese to bedding, cologne and sunburn treatment. In the short season that the elder flowers it must be picked and dried or used fairly quickly otherwise it taints. As for the berries, they are traditionally used for brewing and once cooked can make a lovely addition to jam or coulis. My Irish grandmother used to keep flies out of the kitchen with elderflower (or perhaps it was the smell of her burnt cooking that kept them at bay). Elderflower can be found all along the hedgerow and offers a beautiful scent, delicate and soothing. The berries are noticeable in early autumn, but by the time mid September comes the devil will have spat on them and they will be beyond their best.

Ingredients

4–5 elderflower heads in full
4.5 litres cold water
650 g loaf sugar
2 tablespoons white vinegar
1 unwaxed lemon called Colin; yes Colin the lemon

Method

Dissolve the sugar in a small amount of warm water and set it to one side to cool. Don't put it in the fridge, just allow it to cool naturally. Give Colin a damn good squeeze, and cut him into quarters and remove the rind. Put the rind into a jug along with the elderflower. Add the white vinegar and then add the water (cold). Leave for about four days and strain through a clean muslin bag and bottle in clean screwtop bottles. Within six to ten days it should be ready, but have a taste after six days to see that it isn't turning into just fizz. If it isn't fizzing up enough leave it for another six days and retest.

ELDERFLOWER WINE (STILL)

I think that a number of people feel this is the most traditional of the elderflower wines. I have been offered this more often than the sparkling. Equally I have always felt that the sparkling elderflower is more of a summer drink, whereas the still can be drunk at any time. It offers a light, crisp taste very similar to a Côte du Rhone, slightly lemony and a nice pale yellow in colour. To look at it bottled it offers an appetising image. Sometimes you find that a bottle of country wine doesn't always remain in the same genre as a grape variety. But this one does. I often feel that, when you offer a visitor to your home a glass of something 'non traditional' and 'home made', people squint or hesitate at the offer of a strawberry Burgundy or a pea pod Grigio. Yet once they've tasted it, they are often converts.

Ingredients

250 g chopped raisins
4.5 litres water
2 unwaxed lemons

½ litre elderflower petals
1.5 kg granulated white sugar
1 teaspoon tannin
1 sachet of wine yeast and nutrient
1 Campden tablet

Method

For maximum fun:
Now this may sound a little daft but do gather your elderflowers on a sunny day. You will need to be able to smell the very delicate and distinctive elderflower scent. A good tip is not to collect them at midday as the flowers stop giving off their natural oils. You can't smell the scent but you get maximum flavour and body if you pick the heads at early evening. If I was collecting in, say, later May, I would look at doing this around 6–7 p.m. On a still day and at early evening the smell should be immense. Next pick the small flowers off the stalks. The easiest way to do this is not to nip them but to drag the stalks through your fingers backwards. Pop the flowers into a clean sterilised bucket and press down firmly. Grate your lemons on to a plate and try to avoid any pith. If you grate on to a plate first you can identify the pith and remove it. You should be boiling your water at this stage and once you have added your raisins and lemon zest pour it over the mixture. Give the mix a good period of time to cool to lukewarm temperature and add your crushed Campden tablet. Many people say cover with a clean cloth but I find this isn't necessary as often the cloth attracts dust and has a habit of falling into your brew. This is because as the steam rises it collects in the weave of the cloth and then as it cools the water drains to the centre of the cloth and then creates a weight and falls in. If you are leaving your mix under the stairs, in a pantry or airing cupboard, these tend to be dusty places and therefore are a hazard to your mix. I always

use a shower cap or tin foil. Leave it to stand for three days and stir at least once a day. After three days add the juice of the lemons and the sugar to the mix, add the yeast sachet and nutrient and the wine tannin. Stir well until you are sure it has all dissolved, especially the sugar. If you are doing this when there is a full moon, look longingly out of the window, scratch yourself a lot and howl with your head arched back. I bet no one will bother you . . . Strain through a muslin bag or clean fine-meshed bag into a clean bucket and then transfer into a gallon demijohn, fit the airlock and leave in a nice warm place. Now this really needs to be somewhere where the temperature is going to be fairly constant. Usually a pantry or airing cupboard is good but an ideal place is next to an Aga or near a boiler so that the temperature can remain constant at around 20–22°C. Leave this unstirred for about five days. After five days syphon off the liquor into another sterilised clean demijohn and leave until the fermentation process has been completed. Again, this is when the rapid bubbling process in the airlock has stopped. If you have one or two occasional bubbles this is normal. Leave it in this second demijohn for around 8–9 weeks, by which time it should have become clear. Add another crushed Campden tablet and give it another 24 hours to settle. Once all this has been completed syphon off into sterilised bottles. This wine has one of the finest flavours and most distinctive bouquets I've ever tasted and experienced. I've always found with this particular wine that because of its light, crisp nature it never gives me a hangover.

GREEN TOMATO WINE

I find that living in the country, the swapping of items is commonplace. Sometimes it's difficult to draw a barter to a conclusion. How much is a chicken worth in relation to a cauliflower? And always in the harvest time there is food in cheap abundance.

People are so keen to offload a tree full of fruit, or half a lamb (God knows where the other half goes, I often imagine half a lamb wandering around a field.) But life in the countryside is like this. Many years ago I had someone offer their daughter's hand in marriage. What crossed my mind was what the official level of bartering was for a daughter and if it was her hand in marriage that was on offer, that's a lot of potatoes to have to find.

One of the noticeable items on offer at this time of the year has to be the green tomato. After a cool summer and a wet one as well, many people find themselves with an abundance of the dreaded 'green tommy'. Now if you speak to someone about what to do with them, you will always be offered the advice of turning them into chutneys. At times you can have too much of a good thing and, to be honest, green tomato chutney isn't a favourite on Planet Craig.

When an old lady from the village overheard our conversation about the green tommy in the White Bull, she offered her advice (in return for a beer for her help and assistance). She explained that as a child her grandmother made wine from green tomatoes. So here is a woman in her eighties whose granny had had a recipe handed to her. She offered to write the recipe down on two conditions: one, she needed another pint; and two, she wanted a bottle when I'd finished brewing. Several weeks later when I met up with Mrs Moss, sat next to the fire, she took my offered pint of bitter and slipped me an envelope over the table and smiled.

Ingredients

1.5 kg green tommies
1.1 kg white granulated sugar
4 lemons

4.5 litres water
1 packet of wine yeast
910 g raisins
1 Campden tablet
1 teaspoon yeast nutrient
½ teaspoon pectin enzyme
15 g root ginger

Method

Collect your green tommies and give them a good wash, chop them and place into the fermenting vessel. Then add your water and add all the other ingredients with the exception of the yeast. When you add the four lemons make sure that you only express the juice. You don't want the pith, zest or pips. Just the juice! Give it a good stir and allow a short amount of time for the sugar to dissolve before continuing. Leave this to one side and allow it to stand overnight.

Open the sachet and sprinkle the contents over the mix and then stir well. Give the primary vessel a stir daily with a non-metal spoon and do this for 5–6 days. Check the specific gravity daily and wait until it hits the 1.040 mark. Next, strain your mix through a fine meshed bag like a plastic or a muslin one. Now throughout this book I have mentioned about forcing and not forcing the contents through the bag, depending on what ingredients you're working with. Well this is one that you can get down and dirty with. Either use the back of a large spoon or your clean hands (or your hands in disposable plastic gloves) are just as good. Allow this to settle for a couple of hours and then syphon off into a secondary fermentation vessel and fit a clean airlock.

Now if you want this to be a sweet wine, you should siphon the mix at three weeks. Then add around half a cup of white granulated sugar dissolved in a cup of wine – but make sure the sugar has all dissolved before stirring it gently into the mix. You should repeat this process every six weeks until the fermentation process stops. Syphon every three months until the wine is a year old. Throw a lavish birthday party for the wine and then bottle.

If you want a dry wine it's a lot easier, don't add sugar. But you should syphon every three weeks until fermentation stops, and then every three months for at least a year before you bottle. It's not the easiest of wines in the sense that there is a lot of fiddling and waiting. But after a year its taste is worth waiting for. Imagine a warm sun, kissing a shoreline where clear blue water is gently lapping, and a golden tanned girl walking slowly towards you, her sarong swishing revealing a slightly muscular thigh. Well, it's not a bit like that at all. But it does taste good.

POTATO WINE

Now I'm not telling you to distil your own *poitín* (spud whiskey) but I will tell you how to make spud wine. The nice thing about this wine is that you can use any old potato and it's a great way of using cheap or old potatoes. Sometimes when there are loads of small spuds that won't be bought because they are too fiddly to peel, then spud wine is the one for you. Wilja, King Edwards, Anja or even Nadine are great all-rounders. If you do leave this particular wine for over a year it does have a tendency to grow in strength . . . like whiskey.

Ingredients

- 1.5 kg spuds
- 1.5 kg granulated white sugar
- 1 mug cold black tea

1 teaspoon citric acid
1 teaspoon yeast nutrient
1 Campden tablet
some potassium sorbate
4.5litres water
250 ml grape concentrate

Method

Wash your spuds and make sure you cut out the eyes and any green unpleasant bits. Don't forget that if you leave the skins on this will improve the flavour, giving it a depth that you won't get with just the pulp. Now when you do chop your spuds up I recommend that you grate them first, therefore getting an even distribution of flavour in your mixture. A word of advice: if you wash the starch off the potatoes before proceeding you will allow the potatoes to mix in evenly. A heavy contaminant like starch can compromise the fermentation process. A second word of advice: once you've grated them and washed the starch off, cover them with water otherwise they will quickly go brown as the air gets to them.

Place some water on the boil, add the potatoes and cook for a quarter of an hour. You should find that a greyish scum will rise to the surface. Remove this and throw it away. After 15 minutes, sieve through a fine strainer directly into a clean sterilised bucket. Add all the sugar and make sure it's all dissolved. You should now add four litres of water and leave it until the morning. Add all your ingredients, in no particular order, to the mix and give it a stir whilst whistling the German National Anthem. Pour into a sterilised clean demijohn, add your airlock and leave it be until it settles. The reason I say leave it to settle is because you will find it will froth like mad and you might fear for your safety. Don't worry it's all natural. Once this has stopped, add water to the start of the neck of the demijohn and replace the airlock. When the fermentation process has stopped, or at least slowed down to only a few bubbles passing through the airlock, you can test the wine. Use a hydrometer – or, best of all, take a small glass full and supervise the taste in your mouth. If it's tasty add the potassium sorbate and Campden tablet and leave it to clear on its own. When all the mixture is clear you can syphon into a clean second demijohn. You can always sweeten it if it's too dry, but for me a spud wine should be dry. Leave it a couple of weeks then add another Campden tablet and then bottle.

ROWAN WINE

Rowan is a fairly common surname in parts of the North of England. Many folk are aware of the name but not what it actually refers to. I have a Rowan tree in the garden, which is sometimes referred to as a mountain ash. It is a small tree common throughout the United Kingdom. There are references to the Rowan tree and her berries in a variety of accounts right back to the Middle Ages. Many documents refer to her berries being used in a variety of ways, wine included. The Rowan berries are not-so-much poisonous but they would give you an upset tummy if you ate them. Therefore they should be picked in October – and guess where I have been today? In between dodging the hailstones and rain I have been filling my hat with lovely robin-red Rowan berries. If you leave them into the next month the devil will have spat on them and they will be mushy and you can't use them then. Nature always provides so long as you eat seasonally and work with her.

Ingredients

1 kg ripe Rowan berries
2 litres boiling soft water

2 oranges
1.3 kg white granulated sugar
Some yeast extract

Method

You should pick your berries when they are ripe. You can tell if they are under-ripe, as not only will they be firm to hard but when you give them a squeeze you should find a little ooze at the crown of the berry, similar to that of a rose hip. Remove all the stalks and give the berries a good wash, then place into a clean plastic bucket. Pour your boiling water over the berries and leave to mush for at least three days. There will be a rather distinct smell but don't be too put off by this, and don't worry, it's normal. Stir daily and then strain through a clean muslin cloth into a clean sterilised demijohn. Next you want to make up the sugar and water into a syrup. Use around 850 ml of soft water with the full amount of the sugar, bring to the boil and allow to turn into a syrup, then pour into the demijohn. Grate your oranges and squeeze the juice and add these into the demijohn. Start your yeast off fermenting and add to the wine. Use a big bung of cotton wool in the neck of the demijohn and leave for three days minimum. After three days put a new clean airlock in the neck and leave for about four months. You will find that the wine clears really quickly. After four months syphon the wine off into a clean sterilised jar and leave for at least another six months. You will find that this wine improves with age, but leaving it for as long as you can will improve its body. This is a long process for wine-making but once you have started some and waited almost a year, if you like it, keep the process going and you will always have delicious wine throughout the year.

HONEYSUCKLE WINE

Honeysuckle has to be one of my all-time favourite flowers, not just its shape and its prolific aroma but because it makes a lovely honey if you can confine the bees to those flowers. Honeysuckle is so beautiful but is also very poisonous; such a delicate flower that is such a monster. You should always pick your flowers in the early morning or late evening. This is when the natural oils in the flowers are at their height and are at their most buoyant. The berries are poisonous and the flowers can be upsetting also, so do take care.

Ingredients

1.2 litres honeysuckle flowers
2 oranges
225 g raisins
1.3 kg white granulated sugar
4.5 litres cooled boiled water
1 Campden tablet
1 teaspoon yeast nutrient
Wine yeast
1 cup black tea
1 teaspoon pectin enzyme
2 teaspoons acid blend

Method

Wash your flowers and be careful with them as they are quite delicate, especially if you've picked them one day and are not using them until later. The flowers will become loose and lose their oils and flavour if not used straight away. Use cold water to wash as otherwise the oils will be lost and you will cook the flowers and ruin the fermentation process. Transfer the washed flowers to a clean plastic bucket and add all the cooled boiled water, including all the ingredients with the exception of the yeast. Stir the mixture until all the sugar has completely dissolved. Now leave the bucket for at least 12 hours and then add the activated wine yeast. Stir twice a day, evenings and mornings for the next four days. Strain the mixture, getting all the mix through the bag but never press with this one. Allow to drip slowly because, if you pass it through, it will become cloudy and will spoil your lovely wine.

You should now transfer the strained mixture to a clean demijohn complete with a clean airlock. After six weeks, syphon the wine off. Fermentation will have stopped by now, the air bubbles in the airlock will have slowed down or stopped completely. Sometimes there is a little natural cloud in the vessel so it's advisable to syphon a further two or three times over the next year until it is completely clear. After a year you should bottle and leave for a further six months before drinking. It's a long one this, but all the better for laying down.

There's something of the naturalist, the environmentalist and the conservationist in me, but all in all I think it's the show-off in me. I really like pulling out a pea pod Burgundy, a hedgerow port or a honeysuckle wine. I just feel so pleased with myself when I can offer my friends and guests something completely different.

LAVENDER WINE

This is a nice wine to make and drink. I've always used lavender wine in the same way you would Pimms. A hot summer's day, a long glass and lots of ice cubes and this very distinct flavour that lavender wine has. I don't think this is a general-purpose wine. It has a distinct flavour all to itself, pleasant but not to everyone's taste I would say.

Ingredients

For this fine wine:
1 tin white grape concentrate
1.2 kg white granulated sugar
4.5 litres water
Yeast nutrient (about 1 level teaspoon)
Wine yeast
Half a lemon (unwaxed)
130 ml dried lavender heads, not the stalks

Method

When you come to pick your flowers you can either do this from your own garden in late summer when the bees have finished with them, or you can buy dried all year round. Your own will need to be dried before they can be used. You can dry them in a number of ways. Laying them down on an old newspaper will absorb the moisture, but hanging them on a fireplace or Aga, or laying them on a radiator or even in a warm airing cupboard will do. If you do buy them dried, make sure they have not been scented and are natural. Often they have a lavender oil or powder sprayed on them to enhance and prolong the smell. This will damage your brew and make it taste like bath water: soapy, with a rubber duck floating in the middle.

When the time comes to make your lavender wine and you are wondering what is the best way to remove the heads of the flowers, try running them between your fingers, but up the flower. You will open the flower head slightly whilst at the same time removing the complete heads without getting a lot of unnecessary stalk in there as well. If you go with what would be the logical approach of running the heads downwards and with the growth of the head, you will actually close the heads and leave yourself with several stubborn heads unprepared to be removed. It is always a good idea when removing heads to do it over a tea towel or an old newspaper. The tea towel is better as it offers more resistance and prevents the heads from making a brief escape. Now pour your boiling water over your lavender heads, add the finely and evenly chopped lemon and leave to stand with a cover over it for around three hours. You should then remove the lemon, and leave it to stand again for a minimum of three days. I find it's a lot easier to remove the lemon if you place it into a small muslin bag making it like a lemon bouquet garni. Leave the bouquet garni on a piece of string, but only use string that is natural and not man-made. Blue plastic/nylon string will only colour your wine the most unnatural of colours.

Strain the mixture into a clean demijohn. Next dissolve your sugar in hot water and then add it to the fermentation vessel. Add your grape concentrate, the yeast nutrient and the wine yeast once it's activated. Fit with a clean tight airlock and leave to ferment. If you find that through fermentation the liquid level has dropped, then top up with water – don't be afraid, as I know some people are. After the fermentation process has stopped, decant into bottles and store for around six months and then drink on a hot sunny day.

Hot sunny day not provided.

HAW WINE

As the end of October draws near and the vegetation in and amongst the hedgerow looks bleak, I always think of the birds and wildlife that depend on this part of nature's larder. To the trained eye there is a lot going on in the hedgerow, but I feel strongly that it's not my place to harvest for my own luxury the foods that the countryside creatures depend on for their survival. As I write there is a glut of haws in the hedgerow. These are those very red berries that are usually in seen in abundance but are seldom used and tend to be the last things to be eaten by the wildlife. If there are plenty of berries then you can make a rather splendid wine. This wine will certainly give you something to do over the winter months. And once it has come to fruition the following winter you will warm to its mellow flavour whilst you start this year's brew.

Ingredients

2 kg nice red ripe fat haw berries
1 lemon
2 oranges
4.5 kg white granulated sugar
1 packet wine yeast
4.5 litres boiling water

Method

Give your berries a good wash in plenty of cold water and try not to damage them. Next place them in a large bowl and cover them with boiling water. Put a cover over the bowl and leave to stand for at least a week, giving them a comforting stir once a day. Place your thin rind or zest into another bowl and strain the mixture on to the citrus fruits. Remember unwaxed fruits are better than the cheaper waxed varieties. Unwaxed won't interfere with the process or flavour. Wax adds to the process and leaves a nasty film in the demijohn which can bung up the airlock and trouble the fermentation process. Add the sugar to a little water and dissolve thoroughly. Then add it to your mixture. Stir it in well and when the mixture has cooled to room temperature add your yeast, cover and leave alone for at least 24 hours. Swap vessels, placing the mix into a secondary vessel (clean), add the airlock and wait for the fermentation process to complete. Syphon off and bottle. Leave for six months for the perfect pink winter warmer.

NETTLE WINE

Up in a little seaside village in Lancashire called Heysham, near Morecambe, I found a shop making alcoholic and non-alcoholic nettle beer. It was to die for, a dark brown nutty beer with a hint of raisins. Nettles, as you might know, are in abundance all over the countryside. They are nature's little medicine chest, being used for a multitude of things. Now after my run-in with the beer makers of Heysham I decided to look at making a nettle country wine. This is a sweet wine – you can control the sugar content but the plant itself has its own high levels of sugars, so getting the balance right can be tricky at times. Pick your nettles from the top of the plant and never after mid summer as by then they will be over and woody. Never pick from the bottom of the plant – dogs have generally peed on them.

Ingredients

2 unwaxed lemons
4.5 litres water
1.7 kg white granulated sugar
2 litres fresh nettles
10 g bruised root ginger
1 packet of yeast extract

Method

Wearing gloves for your own protection, wash your nettles in lots of cool water and then drain. Bruise your ginger; a rolling pin is good for this, or a small toffee hammer, or just the palm of your hand. Add it to a bowl or vessel with the lemon zest, water and of course your nettles. Bring to the boil and quickly drop to a simmer for a little under an hour. Pass through a sieve, add the sugar and stir until it has fully dissolved. Place into a clean bucket or holding vessel of some sort. Top up your mixture to the full 4.5 litres with water and wait until its temperature reaches 21°C. Add your yeast extract and mix in well.

Place a cover over it and leave in a warm place for at least four days. After that give it a stir. Transfer it to a fermentation vessel, place a clean airlock on it and leave it to sulk for eight weeks. It should become clear by then. Siphon, and then bottle. Leave for around four months and then get blotto.

PEA POD WINE

Several times in this book I've referred to the famous pea pod Burgundy. When I first heard of this 'product' I was a youngster, naïve and terminally stupid. I loved the BBC comedy programme *The Good Life*, and I especially loved Felicity Kendal. I was very impressed with the idea of recycling, of self-sufficiency and working as a team together with my wife. My downfall was the fact that I was 13, lived with my parents, didn't have a girlfriend nor could find one who looked like the love of my life, Felicity Kendal. I also didn't know what a pea pod Burgundy was.

Over the years of messing around with wine beer and mead I found myself tampering with the pea pod. One of the nice things about pea pods is that the Burgundy can be viewed as a clever bi-product. I always plant up a good selection of peas to be grown and developed over several weeks of the summer. Peas will be eaten, turned into soups and frozen for the winter months. And as a secondary product, where most people ditch them, you can turn the pods into a fantastic wine.

You will always find the beauty of fresh peas over tinned ones is that they are tremendously sweet, and that's because the pods contain a large amount of natural sugar.

Ingredients

About 900 g pea pods
2 unwaxed oranges
1 kg granulated white sugar
4.5 litres water
280 ml strong black tea
450 g sultanas
1.5 ml citric acid
Some pectin enzyme
Wine yeast
Wine nutrient

Method

Wash your pea pods in plenty of clean fresh water as you will always find little slugs and earwigs camping out in your pods. Then trim them all up into evenly sized pieces. Cover them with water and bring them to the boil slowly, cover and then simmer gently for 20 minutes. Place the sugar into a clean sterilised fermenting vessel along with the chopped sultanas. Pour your strained pea pod juice over the mixture but ensure that, when you are pouring, the juice goes through three to four layers of muslin. Unlike other wines, once the bag has drained you can give the wine bag a good squeeze; it won't make your wine cloudy and you will get the maximum of flavour from your pods. Chuck the pods away and give the mixture a good stir to ensure the sugar has dissolved thoroughly. Next add additional water to make up to 4.5 litres if need be. Next add the acid and tea, place a cover over it and allow to cool to room temperature. Juice your oranges and add to the mix and at the same time add the yeast and nutrient and a few drops of enzyme. Cover with tinfoil or cling film, rather than a lid or a tea towel. Now you will need to place it in a warm place to ferment for a good ten days. Give it a stir once a day.

Using the four-thickness muslin bag that you used before, strain your mixture to remove anything that can't be drunk. All solids and semi-solids should now be removed and the liquor should be returned to a clean fermentation vessel. Add fresh cling film and return to the warm area for a further three to four days and then syphon off into a 4.5 litre jar. I find syphoning is much easier than pouring, as you can shift the sediment when pouring and cloud the wine. When you syphon you have great control by just using your fingers. Keep as much sediment out of the finished wine as possible. If the fermentation vessel has lost some of its liquid, make up with some boiled, cooled water to the neck. Use a clean fermentation airlock and leave to bubble away. Once it has stopped fermenting, bottle and leave for four to six months before tasting.

SLOE WINE

I couldn't finish this book without giving you a recipe that deals with the lovely sloe. You can make sloe wine and sloe vodka/gin (and there's a recipe for sloe vodka/gin in Chapter 6).

Sloes are the fruit of the blackthorn tree or bush. The reason why I say bush is because often the 'trees' in the hedgerow are cut back in the late autumn by the farmers to make their hedges neat and tidy. Occasionally people believe that trees should look like trees, tall and proud. Left to grow unhindered the bush would be a spindly tree, gnarled and drawn. Even though this tree will look distressed and somewhat ill, it is in fact very healthy in this state, it just doesn't look like it.

As I write this book in late October there is an abundance of hedgerow fruits and nuts available and my wife is busy squirrelling away in the hedgerow looking for things to take. We do have a plan at the weekend to make some sloe wine. We have had the first frost and are awaiting the predicted first snow, so it's best to get busy with the foraging. Remember though; only take what you want, but leave enough for the wildlife to eat. For so many creatures the hedgerows are the supermarkets of the countryside. I've often met people who get the foraging bug and go at it hammer and tongs, collecting lots of things that they are unsure what to do with and after a short period they are thrown away. Try not to waste this valuable harvest if you can help it.

When you venture out to gather your sloes you should be looking for a blue to black berry, round, plump and tart to the taste. You can buy sloes in the shops and I presume these are either forced or cultivated. Wild sloes are just as good but will need further work on them to make them into a perfect wine.

Ingredients

1 kg white granulated sugar
2 unwaxed oranges
A Campden tablet
Wine yeast

4.5 litres water
1.2 kg sloes

Method

Take half of your allocated water and boil your sloes in it for around 20–30 minutes. As they begin to soften, break them with the back of a spoon, either plastic or wooden. Try to avoid metal because you can't always determine or vouch for the quality of the metal and if it has a tendency to be cheap or badly constructed you may well find your mixture tainted and at worst ruined. I try to make this point through the book because wine making isn't a five minute wonder. It takes time. You can ruin a year or sometimes a two years' project merely because of faulty kit.

Once the sloes have reached the correct level of mushiness, strain off the bulk and pour the liquor into a clean vessel of some sort. Next start off your yeast and, whilst it is doing its thing, get your sugar on to boil with the remainder of the water. Ensure it has all dissolved and add the freshly squeezed juice of your two oranges. Crush your Campden tablet as fine as you can and add that. Stir and ensure it is all evenly dispersed. Next allow the liquid to cool to around 18°C, or lukewarm, and add your yeast. Stir it in and leave in a warm place to ferment for around 4–5 days. Remember to cover the container. After this period you should pour it into a fermentation vessel and leave with an airlock on, until it starts to clear and settle. I went to Settle once. It was shut. And it rained.

Give the wine three months before bottling but sometimes a little longer as wild sloes tend to need to age more so than cultivated ones. Bottle, leave in a horizontal position and mark with a label as to the date and batch. Sometimes it's a good idea to make a note of whereabouts you picked this batch from so that you have an idea of a good vintage or poor. I have always found with sloes the longer you leave them the better. Some sloe wines I have made have looked like perfection in a bottle and have tasted like vinegar. And the reason is that I hadn't left them for long enough. For me, two years in the right conditions has always been the right level of time. But wow, when they have matured they are like nothing else I've tried. Some of them take on a liquorice flavour.

Each vintage will take on a different body of its own, and all this depends on the season; hence the idea of keeping a log. Each season will offer you a different wine. In the past I have found that a summer that has been dry with a sudden burst of rain and a return to sunshine will create the perfect conditions for the natural sugars to develop and in turn the most beautiful of wines.

I know I have gone on about the beauty and quality of certain wines perhaps more so than others, but I have found that if you work with the seasons then after a year you will have such a selection to play with.

RHUBARB WINE

One of the nicest wines I have made and tasted is from a fruit that I do not really like: rhubarb. I was force-fed rhubarb as a child, and told it would be good for me. The biggest lie told by my mother was that it tasted like a Mars Bar. (The same is true of pig's liver – that doesn't taste of chocolate either.) So I grew up hating the plant until, I became older and entered the valley of corduroy and cardigans and started growing the dreaded plant for my wife who loves it. Surprisingly, I was very good at cultivating it, all I did was ignore it and hey presto, I'm a member of the magic circle. My neighbour told me of a perfect end for my garden enemy, wine. And the nice thing was that it didn't taste of rhubarb. You will find that some rhubarbs will shoot in late spring and early autumn. Try to avoid the autumn rhubarb as it doesn't have the same sugar levels and can taste somewhat woody. Go for the spring one.

Ingredients

1.25 kg white granulated sugar
1 sachet wine yeast
2 Campden tablets
4.5 litres water
1.25 kg rhubarb
2 cups of tea (one for the wine and one for yourself)

Method

It's always important to remove any dirt from whatever you are using but certain fruits require a certain approach. Don't rinse your rhubarb in water, as the warmer the water the more destruction will occur of the natural sugars. I've always found that by using a clean, damp tea towel and working the cloth up and down you can easily get into the grooves where any dirt maybe squatting. Importantly, do not peel the rhubarb as the sugars lie just beneath the surface and the peel can be used complete in the wine. Next chop your rhubarb up into small pieces, cover with your sugar and leave overnight. Always cover the vessel if you can, not to enhance the fermentation process but to keep anything nasty and unwanted out. In May, leaving chopped rhubarb and sugar in the open is a recipe for wasps and bees to pay you a visit. When you return to your mixture the sugar should have dissolved completely. If it hasn't, just add a little cold water and stir gently. The syrup that now lies in the container should be removed and retained. The rhubarb should be gently washed with water to rinse away any remaining syrup. Add this liquid to the syrup and make the total amount up to 4.5 litres with additional water and a medium-sized cup of black tea. Next add your wine yeast and then once fully dissolved, pour the liquor into a clean demijohn, fit a clean airlock and leave to ferment. By this time you should know how fermentation arrives and finishes. Watch the bubbles in the airlock. Now, using your hydrometer you should stop the fermentation process by using a couple of Campden tablets. But only consider this when fermentation reaches around the 1.01 mark. Don't be tempted to rush it.

Stand the wine in a place where it's not necessarily in direct sunlight but more importantly, where clumsy hands won't knock it and where idiots won't keep moving and rocking it to see how it is. Leave it under the stairs or in a study or cupboard away from prying hands and minds. Leave it to clear naturally. Your next job is to syphon (not pour) the wine off into clean sterilised bottles, and leave for around 12 to 16 weeks. This is a lovely wine that does improve with age, but is a beauty after 4–6 months. It's a nice touch at Christmas when rhubarb thoughts have long since passed.

WASSAIL WINE

Talking of Christmas (and winter is nipping at my heels here in Lancashire), I couldn't finish this book off without including a wine that is full of Christmas spirit and joy. Harking back to the pre-Victorian idea and ideals of Christmas, wassail and wassailing was a major part of the Anglo-Saxon calendar. Wassailing falls into two major areas: tree wassailing and door wassailing. The orchard version involves men with lit torches of brush walking around the orchards, singing and drinking and wishing the trees well for the following year's harvest. It is believed that the origins of this are pagan. Door wassailing is a revisiting of the tradition of the Middle Ages when the lord of the manor would give food and drink to the peasants in return for their goodwill. This later developed into the carol singing tradition we have today. The wassail wine was and is a spiced wine to keep the warmth in and the cold at bay. These days people wassail as early as July and August as soon as the advertisements come on television telling us we only have 158 shopping days to go.

Wassail wine, is as I said, a spiced wine but you don't have to wait until Christmas to drink it, it's very refreshing all year round. If you want to imagine the glorious smell of it, then Glühwein would be the nearest example.

Ingredients

2 unwaxed oranges
1.1 kg white granulated sugar
A small bag of mixed spices
The zest of 2 tangerines or mandarins (grated)
1 tin red grape concentrated
Wine yeast
Wine nutrient
3 litres boiling water, filtered if in a hard water area
Pectin enzyme
1.3 kg dried mixed fruit
Citric acid

Method

If you are going to make this throughout the year you might want to buy some of the spice bags in advance. They will keep well and there are an abundance of them around Christmas shopping time (so from

July to January then). If you fancy making your own you will need a muslin bag and some mixed spices, including cinnamon sticks, nutmeg shavings or chippings, blade mace, crushed allspice and a couple of whole cloves.

Put your water on to boil and float your spice bag in the water with a piece of string attached for easy removal. Drop the temperature to a simmer and then add your mixed fruit, oranges and tangerine/ mandarin zest and allow to simmer for about 10 minutes. Leave the pan to cool before transferring it to a fermentation vessel. Next add your enzyme and citric acid before leaving it overnight. Pass the liquid through a sieve and remove the oranges and mixed fruit. Give them all a squeeze or press with a non-metallic spoon first to get the maximum of juice and flavour out of them. Return your mixed fruit and the spice bag to the mixture. Add your sugar and make sure it has dissolved before carrying on – in fact, it's a good idea to dissolve it in a little hot water so it becomes more of a syrup and then add it, stirring to ensure it is evenly distributed.

Kick-start your yeast and add it when ready, along with the yeast extract and grape concentrate. Now for the next five days it should be covered but will also benefit from a daily stir – don't do it too vigorously though. Next, drain your mixture through a mesh or muslin bag into a clean bucket and then transfer from the clean bucket to the sterilised fermentation vessel/demijohn and fit a clean sterilised airlock. Now, when fermentation has finished, syphon your wine off into bottles and leave until Christmas Day. Serve with a fat turkey, plenty of sprouts and self-satisfied smug smile.

INDEX